DIESEL EN(
MAINTENANCE

Peter F. Caplen

Helmsman Books

First published in 1992 by
Helmsman Books, an imprint of
The Crowood Press Ltd
Ramsbury, Marlborough
Wiltshire SN8 2HR

This impression 1996

British Library Cataloguing in Publication Data

A catalogue record for this book is available from the British Library.

ISBN 1 85223 696 5

Acknowledgements
Thanks are due to the following individuals or companies for their
help in the compilation of this book:
Perkins Engines Group, Peterborough for illustrative work and
photographs readily supplied;
Lucas-Rists wiring systems for illustrations of some of their range of
crimp terminals;
Colin Wright of The Beginner's Cruising School for providing and
dismantling an engine for detailed technical photographs;
Chris Cattrall for supply of several illustrations and photographs,
and for initial motivation.

Picture credits
Line-drawings by Jan Sparrow
Photographs by Peter F. Caplen

Dedication
To Patsy. Always on my mind.

Typeset by Avonset, Midsomer Norton, Bath
Printed in Great Britain by J W Arrowsmith, Bristol

CONTENTS

INTRODUCTION

The diesel engine is by far the most popular form of propulsive power for boats of all sizes, whether power or sail. The reasons for this are easy to see when the diesel engine is compared with its petrol cousin.

For a start, the diesel engine is theoretically twice as reliable as the petrol engine as it has no electrical ignition system which in the marine environment is always prone to suffer from the effects of the damp surroundings. Secondly, gas oil, often known as 'red diesel' is the standard fuel for marine diesels and is very much less flammable than petrol, which is why it is unheard of for a diesel-powered craft to suffer from a fuel tank explosion. This cannot be said of petrol-engined craft as the number of incidents, although fairly low, are depressingly regular.

These virtues alone make the diesel engine the favoured choice of the serious boat owner who regards safety and reliability above ultimate speed. However, also to be considered is the very important fact that the diesel engine is far more fuel efficient than the petrol engine, thereby allowing a vessel with a given fuel tank capacity to travel that much further when powered by diesel rather than petrol. The easy availability of gas oil from boat-yards and marinas also makes refuelling more convenient. Many yards are unable to stock petrol due to the stringent regulations covering its storage which requires the additional heavy expense of installing underground tanks.

The fact that gas oil is generally very much cheaper than petrol – usually around half the price, except where unscrupulous yard owners enjoy a local monopoly and charge artificially high prices – means that boating can be enjoyed on a sensible budget without too many worries about how wide the throttles are opened.

Although many boat owners are unfamiliar with the workings of the diesel engine they often have some idea of the workings of the petrol engines in their cars. This is a good basis for understanding the diesel engine as there is little real difference between the two apart from the fuel system and the lack of an electrical ignition system in a diesel engine. In fact, the mechanics of the diesel engine are basically identical and once the differences are understood it should present few problems to the enthusiastic DIY owner.

This book explains everything the beginner needs to know to keep his or her boat's diesel power plants in good order, how to rectify simple faults and save a great deal of cash on annual service costs. It will also help to fill in any gaps in the more experienced owner's knowledge. Not only does it cover all the basic maintenance procedures, but it also explains the workings of such power-boosting equipment as turbo-chargers and inter-coolers and the way marine cooling systems operate.

Rather than just concentrating on the practical side of things it also takes an in-depth look at the history of the diesel engine and the way that it has developed. This will give the owner a much better overall insight (and hopefully interest) in his power unit than a straightforward workshop manual format could provide. Unlike a workshop manual which explains no more than how to perform certain tasks, this book attempts to provide a basic understanding of the workings of the diesel engine; and while offering step-by-step instruction on practical maintenance procedures it also explains exactly why each job is required.

Several sections concentrate on areas which many owners may not have considered of great importance, such as the care of fuel tanks. I make no apologies for this as these items, which may be unglamorous and unpleasant to deal with, are vital to the efficient functioning of the entire system and therefore the engine itself.

The largest single chapter concentrates on the fuel system and the reason for this is simply that this is where problems will arise due to bad installation or lack of maintenance. If you give a diesel engine a supply of clean air-free fuel it will probably still run even if it is almost totally 'clapped-out', but if you introduce dirt or air into the fuel even a new engine will soon stop in protest.

Much of the practical content of the book is drawn from long experience of keeping ailing diesel engines running on a minimal budget and with the minimum of facilities. However, this can be part of the pleasure of owning a vessel with inboard power and for those of us who must follow our interest on a tight budget it is almost essential. It is a fact that a job completed by the owner, once the necessary knowledge has been acquired, will be of a higher standard than that performed by a service agent or boat-yard as the owner knows only too well that if problems arise at sea it will be up to him alone to find the remedy, and that if a job is performed properly in the first place a problem will not arise later.

However, regardless of the financial considerations of the reader and whether or not he or she chooses to have his or her annual maintenance performed professionally, self-sufficiency at sea and the ability to solve minor engine problems without having to alert a lifeboat is a part of good seamanship.

SUMMARY

Why the diesel engine is so popular:

- Cheaper fuel.

- Greater fuel economy.

- No electrical ignition system to suffer the effects of a damp environment.

- No risk of explosion from fuel.

1
DIESEL ENGINE DEVELOPMENTS OVER THE YEARS

The development of the diesel engine is naturally closely connected with the man whose name it now bears. However, the early development of the diesel engine, like that of most other complex machinery was a combination of the efforts of many separate individuals. This is not to deny the importance of Rudolph Diesel's own efforts and research over many years as he was a first-class engineer in his own right, serving his basic engineering apprenticeship alongside his many peers. His final designs and prototypes formed the first true diesel engines as we know them today. However, due to the lack of effective communications in the nineteenth century there was little chance of liaison between engineers in different countries, which meant that similar discoveries were being made almost simultaneously by engineers with absolutely no knowledge of each other.

The diesel engine was conceived along with the petrol engine over a period of years as an answer to the horrendous inefficiency of the steam engine with regard to its fuel consumption, which was at best only about 10 per cent efficient – in other words, 90 per cent of its fuel energy was being wasted. It had become clear that development of the steam engine had reached its peak and no significant improvements in fuel efficiency would be possible. It had long ago been deduced that an internal combustion engine rather than the external combustion of the steam engine would be the only way to improve efficiency. This would immediately save the loss of heat from which the steam engine suffered when transferring heat energy from the boiler to the cylinder.

At the time, the most conveniently available fuel source for stationary engines was town gas and it was with this fuel that early experiments with internal combustion engines were conducted. The principle of the four-stroke cycle for internal combustion had been furnished by the Frenchman Alphonse Beau de Rochas in 1862; but at the same time in Germany and unaware of the work of de Rochas, Nikolaus August Otto actually built a four-stroke engine which for many reasons could not be made to run smoothly, so the idea was shelved.

In 1876 Otto developed a refined four-stroke engine which incorporated a raising of the internal pressure within the cylinder by the rise of the piston on the upward stroke before ignition. The idea behind this was to try to cut the harsh mechanical noise of engines available at the time by using the compression pressure to act as a damper to the piston at the top of the stroke. This move did indeed dramatically cut the mechanical noise of the engine, but more importantly it was found that the efficiency of the engine was greatly improved. At this point Otto patented the four-stroke cycle in Germany and in fact it is still occasionally known as the 'Otto' cycle, especially by older engineers with more traditional apprentice training.

The next step was to perfect a liquid-fuelled engine which would no longer need to be connected to a town gas pipe. Petrol-burning engines were built which utilized crude carburettors and glowing platinum igniters, but after much experimentation a low-voltage electric spark was used for the ignition system and the forerunner of today's spark plug was born; an idea which incidentally had been tried in Italy some twenty years previously!

Rudolph Diesel as a young engineer began his career with Sulzer of Switzerland building ice-making machines, and his first attempts at engine development were in the form of an improved steam-type engine but using ammonia rather than water vapour as the power source. The advantages were few and the use of a dangerous liquid such as ammonia made further development impractical. He had followed with fascination the developments being made in the internal combustion field and having the benefit of a first-class education and a sound understanding of thermodynamics he turned his attention to his own theories of internal combustion.

During this time in many other parts of the world fairly crude internal combustion engines were being produced for use in factories to power machinery while also being modified for use as marine engines, particularly in fishing boats. Although all of these machines tended to be low revving and produced relatively low power they were vastly more fuel efficient than the steam engine.

Herbert Ackroyd Stuart in Yorkshire had designed a 'hot bulb' engine which many people later termed a 'semi-diesel' and which operated using the four-stroke cycle with fuel sprayed into the combustion chamber at the top of the compression stroke. This fuel was ignited by a glowing hot metal bulb (as the name implies) which had to be pre-heated with a blow lamp for eight minutes before the engine could be started. Once it was running the heat of combustion maintained the temperature of the bulb so that the engine then ran continuously. Although this engine was low powered and very unsophisticated it was built in the thousands for industrial and marine use, where in both cases it could be relied upon to give a long and reliable life.

Improving Fuel Efficiency

Fuel efficiency was one of the main aims of Rudolph Diesel's designs with the ultimate goal being 100 per cent efficiency although as a realist Diesel knew this could not be obtained. He turned his attention back to the many lessons he had learned in his early years and decided that for maximum efficiency an engine would need to run at extremely high pressure. He was impressed with the theoretical efficiency of the four-stroke cycle and set about designing a four-stroke engine with compression ignition working with a cylinder pressure of 300kg per sq cm (4,276lb per sq in). At that time these pressures were only found in volcanoes and bombs so to give his design credibility he halved the maximum pressure to 150kg per sq cm (2,133lb per sq in), but even these figures were considered unattainable and were turned down.

He returned to his figures and submitted a second design with a working pressure of 44kg per sq cm (626lb per sq in) which was accepted by Maschinenfabrik Augsburg (later to become the famous diesel engine manufacturers M.A.N.) who agreed to build an experimental engine to see if the principle would work. With engineering standards at that time being fairly low due to the lack of high-precision machinery it took a great deal of time and experimentation just to achieve an effective seal within the cylinder, but eventually the test equipment was reading pressures on the compression stroke approaching the designed levels.

On the first ignition test in 1894 the glass pressure indicator on the cylinder head exploded due to the unexpectedly high pressure which rapidly developed within the cylinder when the fuel was sprayed in. The rest of the engine was undamaged and at least the compression ignition principle was proved. The engine was redesigned and could be coaxed into life for short periods of time which, although accompanied by violent detonations and clouds of smoke, had proved that a compression ignition engine could work. From then on it was a case of trial and error to improve on the original design.

Over the years the improvements came with each offering greater fuel efficiency,

but the overriding problem was the fuel-injection system which in early engines used an air-blast system requiring a compressor to supply the pressurised air. It was not until the end of the First World War that a satisfactory airless injection system was perfected and put into production.

During the period between the first successful running of Rudolph Diesel's first engine and the end of the First World War there was also progress made with pre-combustion chamber design; what we now know as indirect injection. This was developed by another engineer, Prosper l'Orange, along with an airless injection system which improved efficiency by removing the need for an auxiliary air compressor to feed the air-blast injection system. The pre-combustion chamber was a separate chamber in the cylinder head

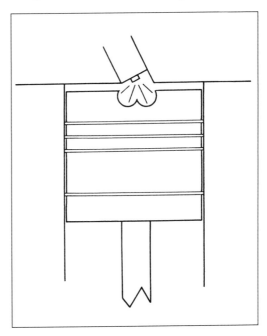

Direct injection. The combustion chamber is situated in the top of the piston.

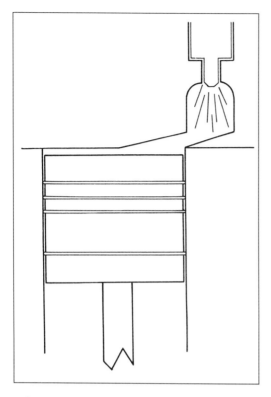

Indirect injection. The combustion chamber is a separate chamber within the cylinder head.

above the cylinder into which air was forced during the compression stroke and where the fuel was injected.

One of the benefits of the pre-combustion chamber design was found to be quieter combustion, although there was a slight loss of thermal efficiency. It was an Englishman, Sir Harry Ricardo, who later perfected the system of indirect injection with his designs of a swirl chamber, which although differing from the early pre-combustion chamber designs in being very much more sophisticated – air is induced to swirl around the specially shaped chamber thereby ensuring a good air/fuel mix and even burn – the concept is basically very similar. Despite being designed in the 1930s the Ricardo Comet Mk V combustion chamber is still one of the most popular designs of swirl chamber among engine manufacturers today.

In 1925 another engineer well known in the field of modern diesel fuel systems was making his name with the successful development of an improved fuel-injection system following the experiences of other engineers. This was Robert Bosch who had already enjoyed much success with his development of magneto spark ignition systems on petrol engines. Bosch fuel-injection systems are used on a wide range of modern engines while the basic design is incorporated into many other manufacturers' products.

The Two-Stroke Engine

In the quest for greater efficiency most early diesel engineers agreed that if a four-stroke engine was reasonably efficient then surely a two-stroke engine with twice as many power strokes for the same revolutions would be doubly efficient. However, this was not the case as the two-stroke engine required an external means of getting sufficient air into the cylinder for adequate combustion. This was provided in the form of a mechanical blower which supplied air under pressure to the cylinder.

The two-stroke diesel became the accepted type for use in large power units especially in ships, where the slow-revving nature of the engine allowed plenty of time for the intake of air and the outflow of exhaust. Not so many small two-stroke diesels were produced, although such notable names as Foden and Detroit Allison were (and still are) very successful with their smaller two-stroke engines. In fact, the Detroit two-stroke is still the standard recommended power unit on many large American cruisers although many British owners tend to opt for four-stroke options for no other reason than that the two-stroke diesel is even more alien to them than the four-stroke.

Recent Refinements

From the late 1920s diesel technology progressed at a steady pace with further refinements being added and greater power being extracted from ever smaller and lighter engines.

Although diesel engines advanced rapidly in the commercial and industrial field and became the standard power unit for ships and commercial craft of all types, it is only in fairly recent times that it has come to be considered the standard power plant for pleasure craft. After the Second World War the majority of pleasure craft were petrol powered and even when mass production of glass-reinforced plastic (GRP) craft began in the early 1960s it was petrol engines which were the favoured unit. No doubt this was mainly due to the fact that petrol engines have always been cheaper to buy than diesels and that petrol was a lot cheaper in real terms than it is now. The fact that small diesels were also significantly heavier and more bulky than

The Perkins Leopard 5 diesel built in 1935 was one of the first of over ten million diesel engines built by Perkins since the company was founded in 1932.

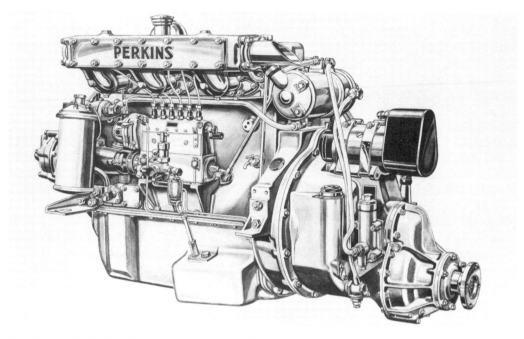

The six-cylinder Perkins P6M of 1952 was (and still is) a reliable and rugged heavy-duty workhorse.

their petrol equivalents probably also affected this decision. The large number of cruising craft around today still fitted with their original petrol engines is evidence of this fact.

Since the early 1970s progress has accelerated at an astonishing rate and with the realization that oil supplies are not infinite, the quest for greater fuel economy naturally leads to the diesel engine. Improved fuel economy brings with it increased overall efficiency which leads to higher power-to-weight ratios. In the last fifteen or so years we have seen the change from petrol to diesel engines in leisure craft designed for serious cruising and more recently even the high-speed express cruiser has gone over exclusively to diesel with almost no loss of performance but a great improvement in fuel economy.

The number of diesel-powered cars on our roads has increased dramatically in the last few years and the staggering performance of many of them as they rush silently down the outside lane of the motorway is evidence enough of the progress made. This progress is now making itself felt in the marine industry with even large planing craft being equipped with diesel power plants as a matter of course.

As we have already seen, early diesel engines were very heavy and slow revving. Compared to such stalwarts of the small cruiser as the BMC 1·5 and 2·2, the later BL 1·8 and 2·5, the Ford 4D and the Bedford 220, all of which were popular with the DIY mariner (and still are to a certain extent), in their turn they too look heavy and slow revving compared with

The latest Perkins Prima M50 is a good example of the advances made in diesel technology in the last sixty years.

the Volkswagen Golf, the Ford 1·6 and 2·5 and the Vauxhall Astra diesels, to name just a few of the latest examples of diesel technology which are now readily available either as ready-to-install marine units or second-hand for DIY mariniza-tion. Their compact size and high power-to-weight ratios indicate the advances that have been made recently in a relatively short time and make the low-cost automotive diesel engine available for smaller and smaller vessels.

In the same manner, the larger engines from specialists such as Sabre and Mermaid who marinize and modify Ford engines are producing ever greater horse-power outputs while manufacturers like Volvo, Iveco, Cummins, Caterpillar and

Perkins are all producing sophisticated power units with power-to-weight ratios which could only be dreamed of a few years ago. With this added power output comes greater fuel economy per horse-power, increased reliability and cleaner exhausts.

While advances are being made in the field of multi-cylinder automotive and commercial engines the sophistication of smaller single, twin and three-cylinder engines is also increasing, although as these are mainly based on industrial engines they tend to be noisier and have less need of a high power-to-weight ratio.

Environmental awareness is an area in which many people are interested, and especially those involved with boating who can see at first hand the damage an oil slick can create or the smog hanging over the land when viewed from the sea. To this end the diesel engine can offer significant benefits in the field of exhaust emissions. It is vastly superior to the petrol engine – even those fitted with catalytic converters. It is only less than perfect in its emission of nitric oxide which is produced due to the high operating temperatures within the combustion chamber of a diesel engine. When combined with air the nitric oxide oxidizes to form nitrogen dioxide. In very high concentrations this can damage the lungs and enter the bloodstream, preventing the blood from transporting oxygen around the body. However, as combustion chamber design improves the problems of even these emissions are being reduced.

As the worldwide demand for diesel engines increases there are sure to be many more improvements to performance, fuel efficiency and exhaust emissions before engineers come to the same conclusion that they did with steam engines – that no further progress is possible!

SUMMARY

- Diesel engine development was an amalgamation of ideas from respected engineers in several countries, finally brought together into a commercially viable unit by Rudolph Diesel.

- The internal combustion engine was the logical progression from the thermal inefficiency of the external combustion (steam) engine.

- Yorkshireman Herbert Akroyd Stuart produced a viable 'semi-diesel' engine which found success in thousands of units used in factories and ships before the first true diesel engine was produced.

- The first test run of a Rudolph Diesel engine in 1894 resulted in an explosion but nevertheless proved that the compression ignition theory was viable.

- Familiar names in the diesel engine and automotive world of today, such as Bosch and Ricardo, are reminders of the contribution their owners made in the field of early engine development.

- Two-stroke diesels can offer greater power and fuel efficiency than four-strokes in the large capacity units built for ships.

2
HOW THE DIESEL ENGINE WORKS

Before looking at the diesel engine in detail it is worth first considering the marine engine itself. In fact, what is a marine engine? The vast majority of so-called marine engines on offer today begin their lives as vehicle or industrial units and are bought directly from the manufacturer by the various marinizing companies for conversion to marine use. They are then marketed as marine engines ready to fit, either as original equipment by boat builders or for replacing life-expired engines by boat owners.

With the high performance demanded from modern craft, the traditional marine engine, with its low revs and heavy build designed to last for years, cannot offer the power-to-weight ratio to satisfy this need. This is one reason why the lighter vehicle engine with high power-to-weight ratio has taken over the market; the other reason is cost.

As we have seen, diesel technology is advancing all the time, with more power being extracted from smaller capacity units which, when carried to extremes, inevitably leads to a shorter working life. However, the modern high-performance diesel when in standard trim offers exceptional reliability and long life, and when fitted in a cruiser will almost certainly last the lifetime of the boat if

maintained correctly at the appropriate intervals.

What we know and accept as the marine diesel of today is far removed from the low-revving heavy monster which has its origins in the earliest of diesel engine designs. The real marine engine is still in evidence in the vastly larger sizes used in ships and the design, though greatly refined, would not be at all alien to Rudolph Diesel.

The Four-Stroke Diesel Engine

The four-stroke engine is by far the most popular of today's small marine diesel engines although two-stroke engines are available from at least one manufacturer.

As we have already seen, the four-stroke cycle (at least in theoretical terms) has been around for well over 100 years and nothing has yet been developed to better it. The cycle is identical for both petrol and diesel engines and the name refers to the four strokes (two up and two down) which are needed to complete one power cycle and which encompasses two revolutions of the crankshaft.

The basic four-stroke diesel engine comprises a heavily built block to withstand the high internal pressures which develop during the combustion process. This contains the cylinders which may number anything from one to twenty or more, although in the smaller sizes which we are dealing with, six cylinders would be a normal maximum and occasionally eight, probably in V formation.

The tops of the cylinders are sealed with a cylinder head which is usually a single unit where the engine is an automotive derivative, but which can also be in the form of separate heads for each cylinder on larger units and heavy-duty designs, such as those used by Gardner engines. The advantage of separate cylinder heads is that work can be performed on one cylinder without the need to disturb all the rest – as happens with engines with a single universal head. The reason for using a single universal head on the majority of engines is of course cost.

Within the cylinder head are passages to allow combustion air and exhaust gases to enter and leave the cylinder. The movement of these gases is controlled by inlet and exhaust valves which open and close at predetermined times during the cycle, and which seal the cylinder during the compression and firing strokes. The opening and closing of these valves is controlled by the camshaft which is in turn driven via either a chain, gears or a belt from the crankshaft.

Within each cylinder is a piston which travels up and down. The gap between the cylinder walls and the piston is sealed with rings of hardened steel which are located in machined grooves in the piston body. The rings are split at one point to allow them to expand outwards and maintain a constant pressure on the cylinder walls. There are usually three or four rings near the top of the piston and one near the bottom. In general, the bottom ring and the lowest of the three or four top rings are usually oil control (or scraper) rings, which instead of being solid steel are in a lattice arrangement.

The grooves in which the oil control rings are fitted have drillings through the piston body so that oil which has splashed or sprayed on to the cylinder walls for lubrication can be scraped off and returned to the sump via the drillings in the ring grooves.

When a piston and rings are assembled and fitted into a cylinder, the rings are compressed by the cylinder walls and the split openings (known as gaps) are reduced to around 0·5 per cent of the cylinder diameter – in a small engine this would be in the region of 0·35mm. Nevertheless, it is very important to ensure that the gaps are staggered around the piston during assembly to ensure minimal cylinder pressure loss when running.

The lower part of the block below the cylinders supports the crankshaft in bearing carriers which are lined with replaceable white metal bearings. The number of carriers and bearings varies with engine make and design; but in general terms for maximum crankshaft support a four-cylinder engine will have five bearings and a six-cylinder engine will have seven. These would be known as a five-bearing and seven-bearing crank respectively. There are exceptions to this flexible rule, one of which is the well known Perkins 4107 and its successor the 4108, which although being four-cylinder engines use three-bearing cranks.

It is the job of the crankshaft to convert the up-and-down motion of the pistons into the rotary motion required to drive the propeller shaft via the gearbox. The crankshaft is connected to the pistons via connecting rods which also use replaceable white metal bearings at their lower end where they are clamped to the crankshaft, and bronze bearings at the top where they connect to the piston via the gudgeon pin.

A sump at the bottom of the engine covers the crankshaft and bearings and is used as the reservoir for lubricating oil. The oil is circulated around the engine after being picked up from the sump by the oil pump and is delivered via the oil filter to all parts of the engine.

The Four-Stroke Cycle

The Inlet or Induction Stroke

This begins with the piston at the top of the cylinder; the inlet valve is already open as it opened just before the piston reached the top of its stroke. As the piston begins its descent down the cylinder it draws fresh air in through the inlet valve which closes as the piston reaches the bottom of the first stroke.

The Compression Stroke

This begins with both the inlet and exhaust valves closed, thus sealing the

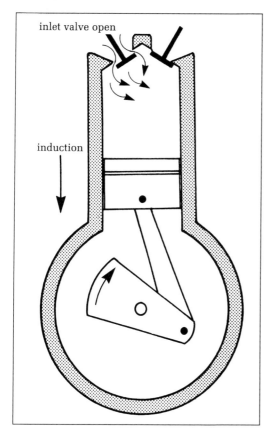

The four-stroke cycle. (a) The inlet or induction stroke.

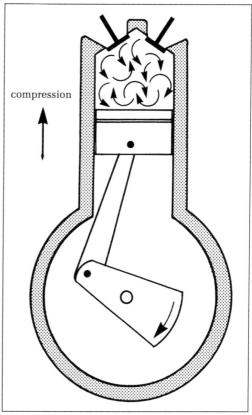

(b) The compression stroke.

cylinder. As the piston rises it compresses the air which was drawn into the cylinder on the inlet stroke. As the air pressure rises the air becomes hotter until maximum compression is reached at top dead centre with the air temperature reaching more than 525°C (977°F).

The Combustion or Firing Stroke

This begins just before top dead centre is reached, as the piston is still rising at the end of the compression stroke. At the appropriate moment just before top dead centre, a precisely metered amount of fuel is injected at a pressure high enough to overcome the already considerable pressure within the cylinder via the injector (or atomizer) in the form of a fine spray. This is immediately ignited by the heat of the compressed air within the cylinder.

As the fuel and air mixture burns, it expands rapidly forcing the piston down the cylinder until just before bottom dead centre when the exhaust valve opens.

The Exhaust Stroke

This begins with the opening of the exhaust valve just prior to the piston beginning its ascent of the cylinder on the final stroke of the cycle. With the exhaust

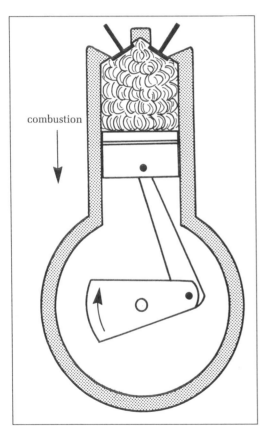

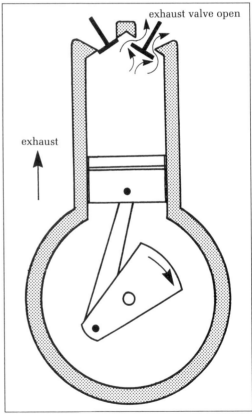

(c) The combustion or firing stroke.

(d) The exhaust stroke.

valve open the piston forces the burnt gases out of the cylinder ready to accept a fresh charge of air on the next inlet stroke.

The inlet valve opens just before top dead centre and while the exhaust valve is still open. This allows the fresh inlet air to be partially drawn in by the last of the exhaust gases and also helps to ensure that the exhaust gases are completely cleared from the cylinder. The exhaust valve then closes as the fresh charge of inlet air is drawn in on the new inlet stroke.

The Two-Stroke Diesel Engine

We will not be dealing in depth with the two-stroke diesel engine as it is not particularly popular with owners and operators of small craft. There are exceptions, however, and this section is included to indicate the differences in operation between the two-stroke and four-stroke engines should the reader ever come across a two-stroke engine or contemplate buying a boat powered by one.

As we have already seen, the two-stroke diesel engine is normally found in large, low-revving ship engines where it really excels itself, and the principle of operation is the same whether the engine is producing 10,000hp or 200hp.

When the two-stroke engine was first conceived the theory existed that as it produced a firing stroke on every second stroke instead of on every fourth stroke of the four-stroke engine it must be twice as powerful as a four-stroke engine of similar bore and stroke. However, additional practical problems were found which negated a lot of the theoretical additional efficiency and the modern two-stroke diesel is now considered to be about one-and-a-half times more powerful than a comparable four-stroke engine.

The biggest problem lay in how to remove the burnt exhaust gas from the cylinder and replace it with a fresh charge of combustion air in the space of one stroke of the piston. The eventual answer was to force the fresh air into the cylinder under pressure from an air pump or supercharger. Being mechanically driven the air pump required a proportion of the engine's power to drive it, and this further lowered the theoretical power output. However, having an excess amount of air forced into the cylinder by a supercharger ensured that exhaust gases were rapidly expelled and a plentiful charge of combustion air was available for the power stroke. This explains the reason why the two-stroke engine is popular in large, low-revving engines. The low revs allow plenty of time for the exhaust gases to be expelled from the cylinder and replaced with a charge of fresh combustion air in the space of one stroke of the piston. As engine speeds increase, the time available for the transference of exhaust gases and air becomes progressively shorter.

Unlike the four-stroke diesel engine which is mechanically almost identical to the petrol four-stroke, the two-stroke diesel is very different to the two-stroke petrol engine used in motorcycles and outboard motors. In fact, it bears more resemblance to the four-stroke diesel: it has a heavily built block which contains the cylinders; the tops of the cylinders are sealed with a cylinder head; the cylinders contain pistons which are connected to the crankshaft via connecting rods; and the crankshaft is located in bearing carriers at the bottom of the block, which is covered with an oil reservoir sump.

The main differences occur in the cylinder head and the cylinder itself. Instead of having inlet and exhaust passages, the two-stroke cylinder head has only an exhaust passage plus an exhaust valve controlled by a camshaft. The inlet passage is located towards the bottom of the cylinder and enters the cylinder at the inlet port in the cylinder wall. The port opens and closes due to the movement of the piston and has no mechanical valve gear like the exhaust valve. When the piston moves up the cylinder the piston body covers and seals the inlet port, and when it moves towards the bottom of the cylinder it uncovers the port.

In practice, the inlet port consists of several openings around the cylinder to allow the admission of as much air as possible in the short time that the ports are uncovered.

The Two-Stroke Cycle

The Compression Stroke

This begins with the piston at the bottom

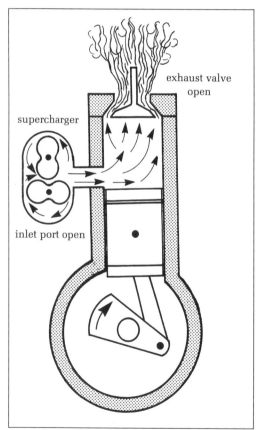

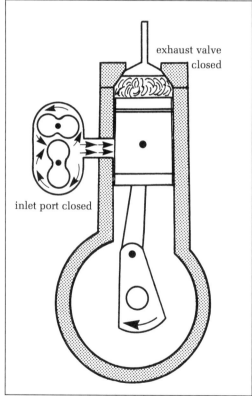

The two-stroke cycle. (a) The compression stroke – fresh air rushes in under pressure to clear the exhaust gases as quickly as possible.

(b) The combustion stroke – the cylinder is sealed by the piston body and the closed exhaust valve is ready for the atomized fuel to be injected into the pressurized combustion chamber.

of the cylinder and the inlet port open as it is uncovered by the piston. The exhaust valve in the cylinder head is also open and a charge of pressurized fresh air is forced into the cylinder to clear the burnt exhaust gas through the exhaust valve and to supply a charge of fresh air for the next combustion stroke.

The exhaust valve closes and the piston begins rising up the cylinder, covering and closing the inlet port. With the cylinder now sealed the air is compressed and the temperature increases rapidly as the piston rises.

The Combustion Stroke

This begins just before top dead centre when the precisely metered fuel is injected into the cylinder and is immediately ignited by the heat of the compressed air. As the air burns it expands and forces the piston down the cylinder.

Before the piston reaches the bottom of its stroke and uncovers the inlet port, the exhaust valve opens and the still pressurized exhaust gases escape from the cylinder. As the piston reaches the bottom of the cylinder the inlet port is uncovered and pressurized air is forced into the cylinder.

SUMMARY

- Today's small marine engines are derived from vehicle and industrial units.

- Spares can always be purchased more cheaply at the local truck dealer's than the marine suppliers.

- Power-to-weight ratios of diesel engines are rapidly approaching that of petrol models with greater economy and safety.

- The four-stroke engine requires two complete revolutions of the crankshaft to complete one cycle while the two-stroke requires only one.

- Theoretically, the two-stroke will be twice as efficient and powerful as the four-stroke, but in practice it is only the large, slow revving types which can demonstrate a marked improvement.

- The four-stroke diesel engine is very similar to the four stroke petrol engine.

- The two-stroke diesel engine is nothing like the two-stroke petrol engine.

3
FUEL SYSTEMS

The fuel system is the most precise and critical part of the diesel engine, yet with simple, regular maintenance is as reliable as any other part. The actual high-pressure working parts of the system which include the injectors and injection pump are beyond the scope of the amateur mechanic to overhaul and repair. This is because they are built to very fine tolerances and require clean, dust-free areas in which to be dismantled if they are to retain their precision performance. However, the work of removing them for service is quite straightforward and will present the DIY enthusiast with no problems. There are many diesel fuel injection specialists and their prices are generally quite reasonable, especially if they are mainly concerned with vehicle rather than marine engines. The fuel-injection systems are identical although prices may not be!

Fuel Tanks

The logical place to begin examining the fuel system is at the fuel tank itself. This may be fabricated from a variety of materials including a mild steel, stainless steel or aluminium. Plastic and fuel-resistant fabric materials are also used for smaller tanks.

Types of Fuel Tank

The mild steel tank has the advantage of being cheap to construct from steel plate, and construction is also within the capabilities of the competent DIY welder using a compact arc or MIG welding plant. Lorry tanks can also be used to good advantage at low cost from commercial breakers' yards.

The major disadvantage of mild steel is the possibility of corrosion occurring inside the tank due to water lying on the bottom plating. If left unattended for several years corrosion will perforate the tank bottom and cause fuel to leak into the bilges. The simple answer is to ensure that water cannot lie at the bottom of the tank for very long – that means a suitable drain valve must be provided in the bottom of the tank during construction. If the valve is opened for a short period every three months or so during the season any water which has collected in the tank will be removed along with any chance of corrosion occurring.

Stainless steel and aluminium tanks are very much more expensive to buy and are less easy for the amateur to construct due to the difficulties of welding stainless steel and aluminium without more specialized equipment. Even professionally built tanks in these materials have been known to split when subjected to high levels of stress in rough seas. Their

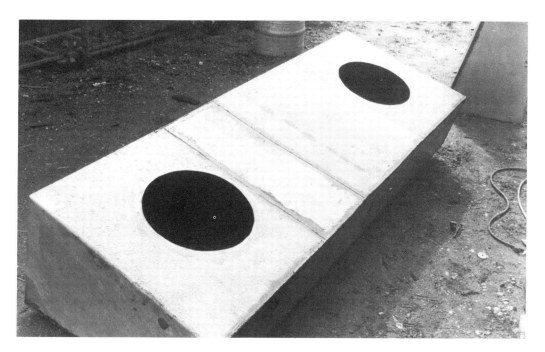

A mild steel tank under construction. Note the large access holes for easy cleaning.

obvious advantage, however, is that they are generally immune to the corrosion problems which affect mild steel tanks.

Plastic and flexible tanks do not suffer from corrosion and are generally reasonably priced. Vetus polythene tanks are popular with many builders of small boats as when installed the fuel level can be seen through the material of the tank thus removing the need for a fuel gauge.

Flexible fabric tanks must be carefully installed to ensure that no sharp projections can snag the material or rough edges chafe it as in either case leakage will be the eventual result.

Water in Fuel Tanks

Water can enter the fuel tank when filling, and many fuel storage tanks used by boat-yards are never cleaned and always have a quantity of water in the fuel stocks. This is passed on to the unsuspecting boat owner when filling the tank. A case in point was the Richard Branson *Virgin Atlantic* Challenge for the Blue Riband when the fuel taken on board during mid-Atlantic refuelling was found to contain large quantities of water. This needed constant filter changes and the eventual need to dry and re-use old filters after all the spares had been used.

Another source of water in the fuel tank is condensation. This is especially prevalent during the winter lay-up when relatively large quantities of water can be produced. The answer to this particular problem is to fill the tank to the brim at the end of the season thereby leaving no room for condensation to form. There is also a bonus in following this sensible practice in that the first tank of fuel for the new season is bought at last year's price, and as diesel fuel does not 'go stale' after a few months as petrol does, there are no problems in doing this.

Whatever precautions are taken to prevent water from entering the tank it is inevitable that some will find its way in by one means or another and this makes it essential to arrange a convenient method of draining. It is therefore not only the mild steel tanks which require draining as water will collect in any type of tank, and although water may not be able to corrode the bottom of stainless steel or aluminium tanks it will damage the precision fuel-injection equipment if allowed to get that far. Good fuel-filtration and water-separation units will protect the fuel-injection equipment, but they will themselves become blocked quickly if sediment and water are present in the tank in large quantities.

There is also a type of bacteria which will grow within diesel fuel tanks when water is present in the fuel. Once established it spreads rapidly and blocks fuel filters in a short time. It is not easy to remove, but again the simple first step to preventing it occurring is to ensure that water within the fuel tank is removed by regular draining every few months.

When draining water from a tank the fuel and water which is removed can be placed in a clean receptacle and left to stand for a few hours after which the water and any sediment will have settled to the bottom. The clean fuel at the top can then be decanted out of the container and returned to the tank ensuring the absolute minimum of wasted fuel. Draining the tank on a regular basis also removes much of the sediment and debris which collects over a period of time and which enters the tank when the filler cap is removed.

Fuel Tank Cleanliness

Unfortunately, the fuel tank is generally considered the least important part of the fuel system, yet if more attention were paid to its cleanliness, many of the fuel-related engine problems such as blocked filters and worn injection equipment would be prevented from occurring.

It is the boat builders who must accept much of the blame for this lack of emphasis on fuel tank cleanliness, probably because fuel tank cleaning is not considered a very glamorous pastime. However, being stopped in mid-Channel with dead engines is even less glamorous!

In many boats it is almost impossible to get at the tanks for regular convenient draining and it is the exception rather than the rule to find tanks fitted with proper inspection hatches to allow the interiors to be inspected for corrosion or sediment build-up. Drain plugs are more common although many owners are not aware of their existence.

In vessels where the tanks are difficult to get at for draining and it is suspected that water is already in the tank contaminating the fuel there is a fuel treatment chemical available commercially. This is poured into the tank and breaks down the water into microscopic particles which then bind with fuel particles. The combined particles are small enough to pass through the fuel filter, and are then burned with the fuel in the engine with no loss of performance or any ill effects to either the engine or fuel-injection equipment. It is preferable to add this fuel treatment to the tank prior to topping up with extra fuel as the action of pumping in fuel causes the fuel and water already in the tank to swirl around – in so doing this ensures that the contents of the tank are well mixed.

Fuel Tank Layouts

The usual recommendation for twin engines is to have separate tanks with each tank feeding its own engine. The reasons for this are that should one tank split the other tank and engine will not be affected, and by using cross-over valves both engines can run from either tank while the defective tank is isolated. In practice many boats have balance pipes between the tanks which negates this advantage.

The fuel feed for each engine is taken through the top of the tank, via a tube within the tank which extends down to a point an inch or so above the bottom. This leaves room for sediment to settle so that it is not drawn into the fuel line. Occasionally there is a small sediment sump below the feed pipe with a drain cock or plug below and this makes regular

draining a possibility. The drawback with this conventional system is that no matter how well the tank is baffled to prevent excess fuel movement, once the fuel level drops below about 20 per cent of the tank's capacity, it is impossible to prevent air entering the feed pipe during rough weather due to the fuel slopping violently around within the tank. This means that a fuel tank with a 1,000 litre (200 gallon) capacity must always carry 200 litres (44 gallons) of fuel which cannot reliably be used.

The tank system which I developed for my own boat has proved to have many advantages over the more conventional systems although it is basically very simple. The fuel feed to both engines (and the diesel-fired, hot-air heating system) is taken from the top of a small service tank with a capacity of 10 litres (2 gallons). This is situated amidships on the engine compartment forward bulkhead below the level of the twin main tanks which have a combined capacity of 1,350 litres (300

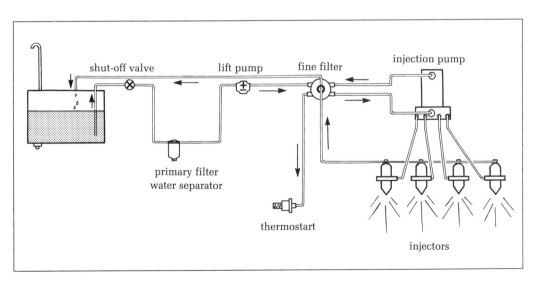

A conventional fuel tank and filter system.

Fuel service tank on the author's own vessel.

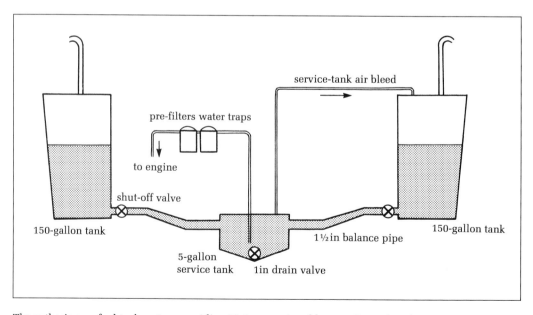

The author's own fuel tank system providing 92·5 per cent usable capacity against the 80 per cent or less of the conventional system.

gallons) and which are situated on each side of the engine compartment. The fuel feeds are incorporated into a small inspection hatch on the top of the service tank so that the interior of the tank can be inspected for corrosion at three-year intervals. Large inspection hatches are fitted to the front face of each main tank so that cleaning can also be performed easily every three years.

The bottom of the service tank is shaped into a V form with a slope towards the front where a 1in gate valve is fitted. Fuel is gravity fed into the service tank via a large bore tube from each of the main tanks and these tubes also act as balance pipes between the main tanks. Gate valves are fitted at the union between the balance pipe and each main tank. When running, the main tank gate valves are closed to a quarter of their normal full–open setting to slow the movement between the main tanks when rolling in rough weather, and in fact, they are only fully opened during refuelling.

There is a fourth outlet on the top of the service tank which is a permanent air bleed back to the main tanks. It is designed to prevent the service tank from becoming airlocked after draining or in the unlikely event of air finding its way in from either of the main tanks during rough weather.

With this system, it is possible to run the tanks down to the last 100 litres (22 gallons) with no fear of air entering the fuel feeds due to fuel slop within the main tanks. This represents a figure of 7·5 per cent of unusable fuel against the 20 per cent of the conventional system.

Draining down is a simple matter which entails closing the gate valves on each of the main tanks, removing the stop plug in the end of the service tank gate valve and placing a large bucket beneath the outlet.

The gate valve is then fully opened and the contents of the tank drained into the bucket. The speed of escaping fuel through the 1in gate valve ensures that most of the sediment and any water are flushed out into the bucket. The gate valve is then closed and the stop plug replaced; this is fitted as a safeguard in case the gate valve should ever leak, and is a standard precaution with large capacity drain valves. The valves on the main tanks are opened last of all to refill the service tank, and the clean fuel in the bucket is decanted back into the main tanks after the sediment and water have settled out.

Fuel Piping

Fuel piping from the tanks is generally run in copper as it is strong, reasonably priced and readily available from bottled gas suppliers and good chandlers. As engines are nearly all flexibly mounted these days it is essential to include a flexible section in the fuel feed to connect the copper to the engine. If the copper tubing is taken directly to the engine, the vibration and movement of the engine will soon cause the copper tubing to fracture.

The flexible tubing must be of the armoured type and not ordinary plastic tube. There is no place for plastic tubing anywhere in a boat's fuel system due to its lack of fire resistance and susceptibility to damage. Apart from the safety aspect no river authorities will allow the use of plastic piping on craft using their rivers.

Successful Compression Joints on Fuel Piping

Compression joints are widely used on fuel systems and are extremely reliable in

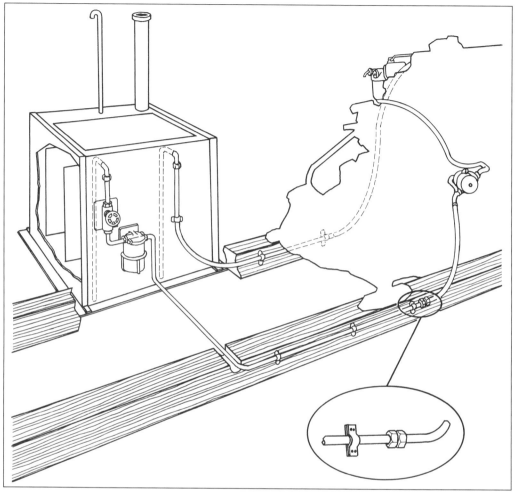

The armoured flexible section of fuel pipe in both feed and return is essential to avoid work hardening and eventual fracture of copper pipework.

terms of fuel-tight integrity. They are simple to assemble and should always give perfect results. However, problems can and do occur when they are in-correctly assembled and the most common cause of problems is over-tightening during assembly.

There are several types of sealing ring (or olive) and they are generally made of copper or brass. The most reliable in terms of effective joint sealing is the copper ring type as the copper is very much more ductile than brass and therefore adapts more easily to the compressive pressure of tightening the nut.

To prepare a joint for assembly the tube end should be cut off squarely, preferably using a proper tube cutter. These are

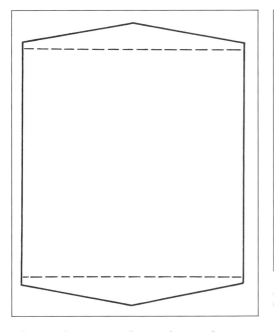

A brass sealing ring (or olive) with tapered ends.

A much softer copper sealing ring with parallel sides.

Brass and copper sealing rings.

cheap to buy and make pipework assembly very much quicker especially where several joints are likely to be required. Using a tube cutter automatically ensures that the end of the tube is cut square while also placing a small chamfer on the end of the tube, thereby making assembly easier. If a cutter is not available a junior hacksaw used carefully will do the job, but the end of the tube will need sanding down to remove all burrs before assembly.

The end of the tube which is to be assembled must be straight as it is vital that the tube enters the joint at right angles. It is therefore good practice to have at least 5cm (2in) of straight tube before any bends are reached. When bending tube by hand it is often difficult if not impossible to begin a bend close to the end of a tube without bending the end itself. A simple solution is to allow an extra 15cm (6in) or so of tube at the end where the

29

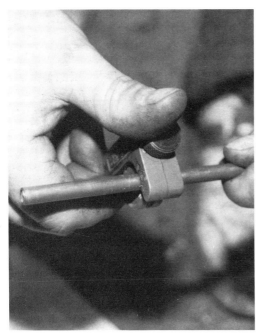 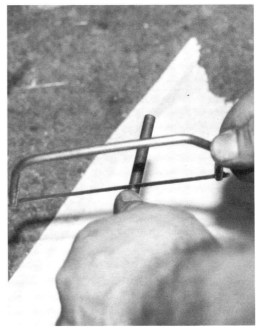

Preparing a joint for assembly. (a) A proper tube cutter prepares the tube end for immediate assembly.

(b) A junior hacksaw used carefully will make an adequate cut, although any burrs on the tube end will need to be removed before assembly.

fitting will be, and after the bend is formed to cut off the excess length leaving the 5cm (2in) of straight tubing between the fitting and the start of the bend.

To assemble the fitting the nut is first slipped over the tube with the thread facing the fitting, followed by the copper ring. The tube end is then slipped into the fitting and pushed up against the flange inside. The copper ring is slid up against the face of the fitting followed by the nut which is carefully threaded on to the fitting and tightened by hand. Tightening the nut with a spanner while holding the joint with another will complete the job, and for small-bore fuel lines sizes this should not require more than about one complete turn to effect a perfect seal. Over-tightening will only distort the ring seal

Assembling the joint. (a) The nut and sealing ring should both slide easily on to the tube indicating that it is free from burrs or distortions.

(b) The tube is pushed into the fitting until it is up against the internal flange. The ring and nut can then be pushed down the tube and tightened by hand on to the fitting.

(c) Use two spanners of the correct size, one to hold the fitting while the other 'snugs up' the nut.

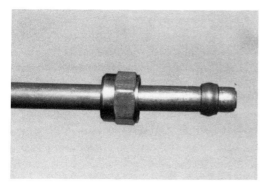

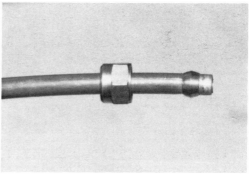

A perfectly formed joint with no distortion of the tube.

A similarly reliable joint, with a brass sealing ring.

An over-tightened joint showing a badly crushed and distorted tube which will inevitably leak.

Repeating the procedure at the other end of the fitting completes the job, providing a neat, fuel-tight joint.

and crush the pipe causing the joint to leak. It is better to under-tighten the joint as it can always be nipped up slightly later if there are any signs of leakage. When a perfect joint has been formed, it can be dismantled and reassembled many times and still form a perfect seal.

Fuel Filtration

The first piece of equipment to consider after the fuel tank is the sedimenter or water trap. It should be mounted as near to the tank as possible so that there can be no chance of the pipework becoming blocked before the fuel reaches the sedimenter.

Sedimenters are designed with an inverted cone over which the fuel flows. Water droplets and heavy particles of sediment sink to the bottom of the unit while the partially cleaned fuel passes out through the centre of the cone. The water and sediment can be drained off at convenient intervals, and electrical sensors are available which will alert the owner when the water and sediment has reached a pre-determined level and should be drained. On many installations the sedimenter is incorporated into a twin-bowl unit with a filter element in the second bowl for removing fine particles of sediment.

From the sedimenter the fuel passes to the engine fuel-lift pump which incorporates a coarse filter, and then on to the fine filter. We will look more closely at the lift pump later.

It is normal nowadays for the fine filter to double as an agglomerator which not only removes the very fine dirt particles remaining in the fuel but also the tiny droplets of water. The fuel enters the unit and passes down through the element

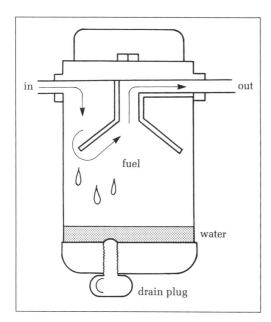

A modern sedimenter and water trap.

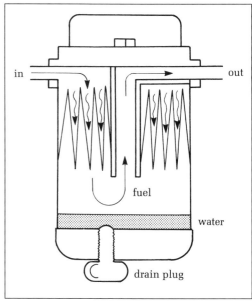

A modern fine filter and agglomerator.

A pair of CAV filter/agglomerators used for heavy-duty filtration and sediment collection.

to this high-precision equipment. It is for this reason that the boat owner should pay particular attention to the cleanliness of the entire fuel system, starting with the tank. Fuel filters are very cheap to buy and take only a few minutes to change, yet they make the difference between reliable long life and constant problems.

Changing a Fuel Filter

As with all engine servicing the best time to change the fuel filters is at the end of the season so that the boat is ready as soon as the first fine spring days occur. For the purpose of this chapter we will be using CAV equipment. It is common throughout the world and is also very moderately priced as it is used on commercial vehicles – this also makes filter elements readily available from car accessory shops.

Sedimenters should have been drained at regular intervals throughout the summer and can now be dismantled and cleaned out thoroughly. The majority of CAV filters, agglomerators and sedimenters used on marine engines are dismantled in the same manner as they tend to use many common parts. There is a central bolt which passes through the head of the unit to the base and which holds the entire unit together.

A sedimenter consists of a head which is flanged for bolting to the engine or bulkhead, a sediment or water trap and a deep base with room for water and sediment to collect and into which is fitted the drain plug. The base may be either glass or aluminium. Aluminium is recommended for boat use as it is less susceptible to damage, but many owners prefer to accept the slight risk of using the glass type as it is more convenient to check for water and sediment without draining.

where water droplets and fine dirt particles are separated. When the fine droplets of water are passed through a porous medium such as the filter element, they combine into larger droplets which pass through the element and sink to the bottom of the filter body. There they can be drained off in the same manner as is used with the sedimenter. The clean fuel passes up through the centre of the filter where it continues to the high-pressure fuel-injection pump.

At the injection pump the fuel is metered precisely and supplied at high pressure to the injectors where it is sprayed into the combustion chamber at the optimum moment, at the top of the compression stroke. Once the fuel has reached the injection pump and injectors it must be as clean as possible otherwise serious and costly damage will soon occur

33

Dismantling a fuel filter. (a) Slacken the central bolt.

(b) Draw the bolt up.

A filter agglomerator consists of a head, usually identical to that of the sedimenter, a disposable filter element and a deep base, with or without a drain plug and made of either glass or aluminium.

A filter is virtually identical to the agglomerator and uses the same element. The only differences are that it utilizes a shallow base and flow is generally in the opposite direction to that of the agglomerator with fuel entering down the central passage of the filter and then passing up through the element. This provides slightly greater element life but offers no water separation protection. It is therefore generally used where excessive sediment and water are not expected to be a problem.

For heavy-duty cleaning, where high fuel flow is required and where longer service intervals are necessary, larger capacity long filter elements are available

(c) Separate the base and filter cartridge.

(d) The rubber sealing ring is carefully prised out of the recess in the filter head.

which will fit any of the previously mentioned units if an extension stud is used to lengthen the central bolt.

Dismantling of all the above units is simply a matter of slackening the central bolt while supporting the base and filter element or sediment trap. Once the bolt is loose the lower assembly may be lowered and removed. The filter element or sediment trap can be separated from the base after which the rubber sealing rings are removed from the recesses in the base and head. Glass-bowl types have an additional seal between the top of the glass and the filter element or sediment trap. There is also an O ring fitted below the washer under the head of the central bolt which locates in a recess; and another around the central locating flange under the head which separates the dirty unfiltered fuel from the clean filtered fuel. All such seals should be replaced with the

(e) The ring in the base is also prised out.

35

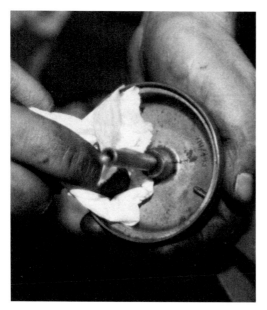

(f) The base can then be wiped out to remove any sediment.

(g) Renew the small O ring beneath the washer on the central holding bolt.

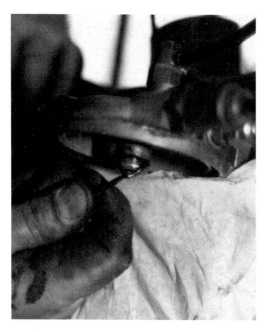

filter, and are supplied for this purpose with each filter element.

There will almost certainly be some sediment in the base of all these units which may need scraping off. The base

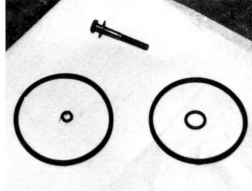

(h) Remove the O ring separating the unfiltered from filtered fuel.

(i) New seals are supplied in the box with the filter element.

can then be rinsed in some clean fuel and dried. The sediment trap should be checked for dirt and cleaned as necessary prior to reassembly.

Reassembly is equally simple although a little care is required to ensure that the rubber seals do not become twisted or kinked. Each seal is located into its recess in the base and head and central locating flange, and for glass-bowl types the additional seal is located around the bottom of the filter element, and the filter and glass are assembled. A new O ring is also fitted under the washer of the central bolt. The filter element is then offered up into the head and will slip over the central flange and seal, to be followed by the base. After this the central bolt is passed through the head and located in the thread in the base. It should first be tightened by

Reassembling a fuel filter. (a) A new sealing ring is located inside the flange in the base . . .

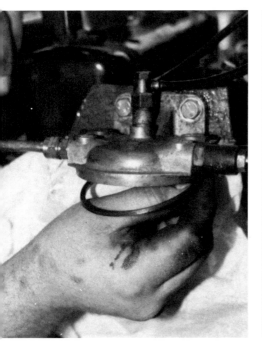

(b) . . . beneath the filter head . . .

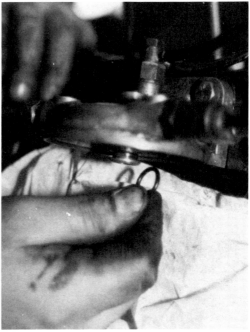

(c) . . . and on the central locating flange.

(d) The new element is offered up with the base and the central bolt is screwed in until hand-tight.

(e) The central holding bolt is 'nipped-up' but not over-tightened.

hand to ensure that it is not cross-threaded, and after ensuring that all the seals are correctly located the bolt may be tightened. The bolt should not be over-tightened but 'nipped up' to bring the seals under pressure, which will ensure air- and fuel-tight joints.

Fuel-Injection Pumps

There are basically two types of fuel-injection systems in common use today, the only difference between them being the injection pump itself which may be either the in-line (jerk) or rotary type.

Both types are used on modern high-speed diesels, although the rotary pump is now more common on the latest small auto-motive diesels. This is because of their lightweight and compact nature and the pump's inherent ability to supply an equal amount of fuel to each cylinder and at the correct moment without adjustment to individual pumping elements. The two types are easy to differentiate as the in-line pump has its injector pipes in a line (usually on the top) while the rotary pump has its injector pipes located radially around a rotor housing at the end of the body.

The In-Line Pump

The in-line pump is in reality a set of separate pumps housed within a body containing a camshaft which drives each pump via its own cam. Fuel is fed into an individual pump at lift pump pressure and as the plunger begins to rise it seals the inlet valve in a similar manner to a two-stroke engine piston. As it continues to rise, the fuel which is now sealed into the chamber under pressure, exerts a force on a delivery valve which is pre-set to open at a certain pressure. The fuel in the pump then passes into the injector pipe and forces the fuel which is already present within the pipe along to the injector. Here the needle valve opens and the fuel at high pressure is sprayed into the combustion chamber.

Meanwhile, the pump plunger continues to rise from the force of the cam until a helical cut-away (or helix) in the plunger clears the spill port. This immediately drops the pressure within the chamber and the delivery valve snaps shut to end injection cleanly. Once the delivery valve in the pump closes the pressure drops in the injector pipe and the injector needle valve closes to prevent any blow-back from the combustion chamber.

The amount of fuel injected at any one time is controlled from the throttle via the fuel rack. This acts on the pump plunger to turn it within the chamber and so adjust the position of the helix and the moment at which the spill port is opened. At tick-over the helix is near to the spill port and therefore cuts off injection very quickly, but at full throttle it is much further away and allows injection to continue for much longer before opening the spill port.

The Rotary Pump

The rotary pump performs the same function as the in-line pump except that it does it in a totally different manner. Fuel is fed at lift pump pressure to the pump where it passes through the transfer pump which raises the pressure to an intermediate level. The fuel is then passed to the metering valve which regulates the amount of fuel passed to the rotor and which is controlled by the throttle and governor. Next, the fuel passes to the hydraulic head and enters a drilling which corresponds with a drilling in the rotor at a set moment. Inside the rotor are two plungers which act as a pumping medium as they move in or out by the action of cam followers operated by internal lobes on the stationary cam ring.

As the fuel enters the rotor the plungers are apart to make room for the entering fuel. As the rotor turns the drillings are closed and the fuel between the plungers is sealed into the plunger chamber. The rotor turns further until another drilling in the hydraulic head which is directly connected to one of the injector pipes corresponds with the drilling in the rotor. When this happens the plungers are forced together by the cam followers acting on the cam ring. This forces the fuel at high pressure out of the rotor and into the injector pipe, and forces the fuel which is already present within the pipe along to the injector. Here the needle valve opens and the fuel, which is at high pressure, is sprayed into the combustion chamber.

As the rotor turns further the drillings no longer correspond and injection ends with the needle valve in the injector snapping shut to prevent blow-back from the combustion chamber in exactly the same manner as with the in-line pump.

Both types of pump can be driven via the timing gears or chain of the engine, while rotary pumps may also be driven directly from the camshaft. The timing of the injection point is dependant on the correct setting of the meshing of the gears or chain. Timing marks are provided on the gears so that the engine crankshaft and camshaft and the injection pump can be aligned for correct engine operation.

Final precise injection timing of rotary pumps is set by altering the position of the pump body in relation to the pump shaft. This is achieved by turning the pump on its mounting and locking it into position with the securing nuts. The holes in the pump flange are elongated to allow for this small amount of final adjustment.

Removing a Rotary Pump

Although rotary injection pumps are mounted in different positions on different makes of engine the method of removal and replacement is very similar for all types. The British Leyland 1·8 engine with its predecessor the 1·5, has proved to be a great favourite with boat owners for many years. This particular engine has the injection pump mounted behind the timing cover and is driven via the timing chain in sequence with the crankshaft and camshaft. The pump shaft is a spline drive with one spline being twice as wide as the rest. This is called the master spline and ensures that the pump shaft can only be fitted in one position in relation to the timing chain.

On the pump mounting flange is a scribed line which should correspond with another scribed line on the engine flange. It does not always correspond exactly as the pump may at some previous time have been overhauled and reset slightly differently internally so that it had to be set up on the engine in a slightly different position. If this is found to be the case then the flange should be remarked before moving the pump, so that both lines correspond and thereby ensuring that the pump is refitted in the same position. Removal is then a straightforward operation.

Before beginning removal it is worth while cleaning the area around the pump and the pump itself to prevent dirt entering once the pipework has been disconnected. Both ends of the injector pipes should be disconnected so that they can be removed completely. Injector pipes must never be bent out of the way as they are liable to snap or become kinked and weakened. In the same manner, if the inlet and return pipes to the pump are in the way they should also be removed completely to avoid damage. Once the pipework is out of the way the pump-securing nuts may be removed complete with washers, and the pump carefully slid away from the engine disengaging the splines in the drive.

The pump can then be emptied of fuel by inverting it, and if plastic blanking plugs are available they should be fitted into or over all the pipe unions and the pump immediately placed in a clean plastic bag to keep dirt and damp out. Plastic blanking plugs are available from diesel engineers who will usually supply a handful if the pump is being taken in to them for service. Once the fuel pump is removed, the gasket between the pump and the engine mounting flanges should be removed and discarded.

Check the position of the scribed line and corresponding marker before disturbing the injection pump.

After removing the injector pipes, fuel inlet and return pipes, the securing nuts can be undone and the pump slid carefully off its mounting.

The Master spline is easy to distinguish . . .

. . . as is the locating slot in the timing case.

Fit a new gasket dry to allow the pump to be aligned precisely with the timing marks.

Refitting a Rotary Pump

When installing the pump after service a fresh gasket should be fitted dry to the engine flange. If sealant is used it will make it impossible to alter the position of the pump to finally line up the scribed lines on the flanges without tearing the gasket.

The master spline on the pump shaft should be positioned so that it corresponds with the position of the master spline in the engine drive. This can usually be seen by shining a torch into the drive or, if the engine is positioned where it is impossible to see into the drive, the position of the master spline can often be found by feeling inside the drive with a fingertip.

With both splines roughly aligned the pump may be offered up into position and turned gently to locate the master splines. It must never be forced as damage may occur, and in any case once the master splines are aligned the pump will slide smoothly and easily into place. The timing marks can now be aligned accurately and the securing nuts tightened.

Removing an In-Line Pump

In-line pumps are usually mounted solidly on the engine either with a flange mounting similar to the rotary pump or with a steel strap. An external coupling is used to transmit the drive from the engine timing gears to the pump and this removes any slight misalignment between engine and pump. As with the rotary pump it is worth cleaning down the area around the pump to prevent dirt entering it before disconnecting the pipework.

With the pump mounting nuts or strap unfastened the pump can usually be lifted away from the engine by sliding the coupling apart. There is no gasket to remove as the drive coupling shaft has its own oil seal which is not disturbed during pump removal.

The pipe unions should be sealed with plastic blanking caps and the pump placed in a clean plastic bag.

Refitting an In-Line Pump

Refitting the in-line pump is slightly more complex than with the rotary as there is no master spline to ensure that the pump timing is automatically set. The engine must be turned until number one piston is near the top of its compression stroke.

This can be ascertained with the injector removed by placing a long rod into the injector orifice to check that the piston is rising, and that the inlet and exhaust valves are closed. Ensure that the rod is long enough so that it will not drop inside the cylinder and that it does not jam between the piston and cylinder head.

When both valves are closed their rockers will have a slight free movement up and down indicating that the valve springs are not under compression and that the valves are therefore closed. If the piston is rising on the exhaust stroke, the exhaust will be closing, indicating that the engine must be turned through another complete revolution before the compression stroke is reached.

The engine manual will indicate where the injection timing marks are located on the engine – they may be on the flywheel at the rear of the engine or on the crankshaft pulley at the front. A fixed pointer will also be fitted which must be aligned with the timing mark by further turning of the engine. If this mark is passed the engine should be turned back well past the mark before turning it forward again. This removes any backlash in the gears or chain which could affect accuracy of aligning the pump coupling.

With this position set the pump coupling must be turned to align the timing mark on the case with the mark on the pump shaft. The pump can now be refitted and the coupling connected.

Ensure that the injector pipes are refitted in the correct places as they will not bend very far without kinking or breaking.

With both types of pump care should be exercised when reconnecting the pipework to ensure that each pipe is run to its correct position. Injector pipes are pre-formed and each will only fit between the pump and the correct injector. If a pipe seems to require a lot of bending it is almost certainly fitted to the wrong injector and pump union.

Fuel Injectors

The operation of an injector is directly controlled by the action of the injection pump forcing fuel under pressure along the injector pipe to the injector. Apart from this the fuel injector has no mechanical drive of any sort.

Removing an Injector

As with the injection pump, an injector should only be dismantled in clean conditions where the appropriate equipment for testing, cleaning, repairing and resetting are available. Without the correct pressure testing equipment to reset the pressure at which injection takes place, the injector will not function correctly and may dribble. This will then cause violent knocking within the engine due to excess fuel entering the combustion chamber and causing excessive combustion pressure to build up.

However, injector removal is a simple task for the DIY owner. Injectors are secured into the cylinder head with two studs and nuts which must be removed by slackening equally. The injector may be reluctant to move from its bore as carbon deposits may have built up around the tip, however, a light tap with a soft-faced hammer around the body will usually free

Removing an injector. (a) A ⅝in open-ended spanner is used to slacken the injector pipe.

it sufficiently for removal. If it is particularly obstinate a bar may be needed under the securing flange to lever it upwards while you tap gently around the body. Ensure that the bar cannot distort the securing studs while you are levering.

Once the injector is removed from its bore check that the copper sealing washer is still attached to the end of the injector body. If it is not it will be found at the bottom of the injector bore and should be hooked out with the end of the screwdriver or similar tool, once again being careful to ensure that the tool cannot drop inside the cylinder.

(b) The leak-off pipe can then be removed carefully.

(c) Slacken the securing nuts equally.

(d) Draw the injector up.

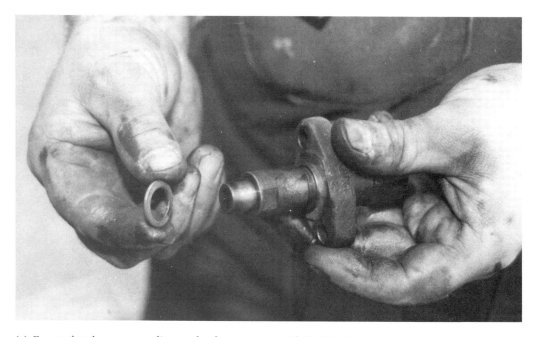

(e) Ensure that the copper sealing washer has come out with the injector.

Refitting an Injector

When refitting an injector the copper sealing washer must be renewed – new ones are generally supplied when injectors are overhauled. If for any reason new washers are not available the old ones may be annealed to renew their sealing properties by heating to a cherry red with a blow lamp (or over the cooker) and plunging into cold water.

The new washer is fitted over the end of the injector body prior to the injector being replaced into its bore in the head. The securing nuts should then be run down the studs an equal amount until they are finger-tight, finally tightening both down equally with a socket or spanner to ensure a gas-tight seal.

If, once the engine is started, there is evidence of blow-by from an injector the two most likely causes are either that the sealing washer has been inadvertently omitted or that the securing nuts have been tightened unevenly.

Fuel-Lift Pumps

Diaphragm-type lift pumps are the most common in small- to mid-range diesels and are a fairly simple piece of equipment. They consist of a two-part body which contains a diaphragm secured around its periphery and which forms a seal between the upper and lower halves of the body. A coarse gauze filter is sometimes located in the upper half of the pump along with the

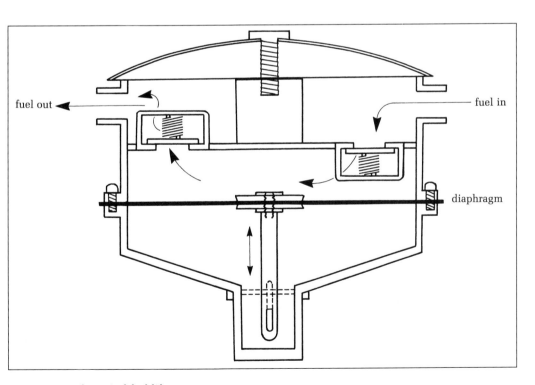

fuel out

fuel in

diaphragm

Cross-section of a typical fuel-lift pump.

A typical fuel-lift pump removed for overhaul. Note the hand-priming lever with spring return nearest the camera, and cam-operated lever to the right and pointing upwards.

simple spring-loaded inlet and outlet valves above the diaphragm.

The centre of the diaphragm is sandwiched between two metal discs attached to a pull rod below the diaphragm. A return spring acts on the lower metal disc of the diaphragm to maintain its centralized position. The pull rod is attached to a two-part operating arm which is pivoted within the pump body and driven from the engine camshaft.

When the operating arm is moved by the camshaft it exerts a downwards pressure on the diaphragm against the spring pressure via the pull rod which causes fuel to be drawn into the chamber through the inlet valve. As the operating arm returns, the spring pressure causes the diaphragm to return to the central position and this forces the fuel from the chamber through the outlet valve.

When fuel pressure on the outlet side

A lift pump partly dismantled for cleaning.

One of the small, non-return valves.

rises to a point where it is greater than the return spring pressure it simply holds the diaphragm down so that no more fuel is pumped until the pressure begins to drop as fuel is used. As soon as there is a small drop in pressure the diaphragm is allowed to move up and pump additional fuel. While the diaphragm is stationary the operating arm continues to move under the influence of the camshaft, but its two-part design means that only the part in contact with the camshaft moves while the part attached to the pull rod remains stationary with the diaphragm.

Should the diaphragm become damaged the pump will cease to operate, and in an emergency a gravity feed may be set up to bypass the pump in order to keep the engine running.

Little maintenance is required for the diaphragm-type pump except to clean the coarse gauze filter once a season during annual maintenance and to remove any residue found in the pump body.

Plunger-type lift pumps operate in a similar manner but are generally located on in-line injection pumps and are driven from the pump camshaft. They would normally be serviced with the injection pump.

Bleeding the Fuel System

Once the fuel system has been disturbed and pipe unions opened it will be necessary to bleed the system to purge it of air. This is a simple job assuming that all the pipe joints and filter seals have been correctly refitted and are effecting a proper seal. If after much priming it is found that air is still in the system it is a fair assumption that there is an air leak somewhere on the suction (fuel tank) side of the lift pump. Any leaks on the pressure (injection pump) side of the lift pump will not cause air to enter the system, but will simply allow fuel to escape – this can be checked for visually.

With the fuel system completely empty after an overhaul, including removal of the injection pump for maintenance, replacement of fuel filter elements and cleaning of the lift pump, it will take a few minutes of manual pumping on the lift pump to fill the system with fuel.

The first task is to slacken all the bleed vents throughout the system. There is usually one on top of the filter, but if there is not the fuel outlet union to the injection pump may be slackened off for this purpose. There are normally two on rotary injection pumps, one on the pump body and one at the top of the governor housing. These will need only one turn to slacken them sufficiently. If they are undone completely there is the danger that they will drop into the bilge and be lost.

Bleeding the fuel system. (a) Bleed vents on a rotary injection pump.

(b) Slacken the outlet union to the fuel injection pump to bleed the filter.

With all vents open the lift pump may be operated. If there is no resistance felt when pumping manually, the operating arm may be resting on the top of its cam thereby preventing the pump from operating. Turning the engine over manually by half a turn will move the camshaft and drop the operating arm, thus allowing manual pumping.

The manual lever should be operated until fuel with no signs of any bubbles is being emitted first from the filter, at which point the bleed screw or outlet union can be tightened, followed by the injection pump bleed unions. If a tray is set up to catch the lost fuel it will help to keep the bilge clean. Once the system is free of air and all the unions are tight, two of the injector pipe unions can be slackened at the injectors to bleed air from the high-pressure side of the pump and the injector

(c) Slacken the vent screws on the injection pump body and governor housing.

(d) Operate the lift pump manually.

(e) Slacken two of the injector pipe unions at the injector ends.

pipes themselves. Although slackening them a couple of turns is sufficient to allow air to escape, it is often worth disconnecting one completely so that the amount of fuel being expelled from the pipe union can be seen.

The engine throttle should be set to maximum and the stop control checked to ensure that it is in the run position. The engine may then be cranked over on the starter while you watch the amount of fuel being expelled from the pipe. If no fuel is expelled or there is only the occasional dribble this will indicate that the injection pump requires further bleeding. If a good charge of fuel is expelled while cranking the engine and smoke is emitted from the exhaust this will indicate that the system is free from air and that injection is taking place. Many direct injection engines will actually start and run at this point with two injector pipe unions disconnected. If this happens the engine should be stopped and the unions reconnected. Indirect injection engines will need the normal cold-start procedure at this point to get them running.

Cold Starting Aids

There are four main types of cold starting aids in general use at the moment.

Heater Plugs

The most popular type of cold starting aid for engines with indirect injection is the heater plug. A separate plug is screwed into each combustion chamber and consists of an electrically operated heating coil (inside the chamber) which warms the air to assist with initial combustion.

To operate, either a button is depressed

for thirty seconds, or in the latest engines an automatic timer does the job after which the chamber is warm enough for the engine to fire as soon as it is turned on the starter. The plugs are not serviceable and they either work or they do not!

To test them on a cold engine simply press the button or operate the timer and after thirty seconds feel each plug to ensure that it is warm. Any that are defective will remain cold. Replacing a defective plug is simply a matter of unscrewing the old plug and replacing it with a new one, although care must be taken to ensure that the old plug does not sheer off as it is being removed. If it does so the cylinder head will have to be removed to get at the broken piece.

Thermostart

The Thermostart is the most popular type of cold starting aid for direct injection engines and again consists of an electrically operated heating coil. However, in this case only one unit is fitted and this is situated in the inlet manifold. As the coil heats up it opens a ball valve which allows diesel fuel on to the heating coil, which bursts into flame immediately the engine is turned on by the starter. The flame is drawn into the cylinders and raises the temperature to ease starting. As direct injection engines are easy to start in most conditions the Thermostart is usually only needed in the coldest of winter weather.

Once again, they are non-serviceable and should be replaced if defective. Testing a Thermostart is simply a matter of operating the switch or button and observing the unit for the smoke which should appear after a few seconds. If left on it will eventually burst into flame showing that it is working correctly. If it

A CAV Thermostart.

remains cold it is either defective, there is a fault in the wiring or there may possibly be a blown fuse.

Early examples of this type of cold-start device were fed from a reservoir which had to be topped up manually, while later models used a small reservoir fed from the fuel return to the tank. However, the latest engines use a direct feed from the fuel filter which removes the need for reservoirs. The Thermostarts themselves are identical and it is therefore perfectly feasible to update early systems to the direct-feed method and remove the additional pipework and reservoirs, thereby simplifying the system.

Excess-Fuel Device

The excess-fuel device consists of a manually-operated button on the side of the injection pump which causes the fuel rack to open past its maximum fuel position. This then allows a large volume of fuel to enter the cylinder on the first turn of the engine. Once the engine has fired it automatically resets itself to the normal run position.

Ether System

The Ether system uses a highly flammable liquid which is sprayed into the cylinder while the engine is being turned on the starter. It is basically the same as the 'easy start' aerosols which many owners of worn-out engines resort to for starting, except that the system is installed within the engine compartment and can be remotely operated. It is generally only used on large, specialized engines and is unlikely to be found on small- to medium-sized marine engines.

SUMMARY

- The fuel system is the most critical area of maintenance, but can be maintained by the DIY owner with regular filter changes and occasional tank cleaning.

- Cleanliness is essential when working on the fuel system.

- Diesel injection equipment can only be repaired and overhauled by specialists with the proper facilities.

- Care must be taken to ensure that water and dirt do not enter the fuel tank when filling.

- Tanks should be topped up at the end of the season to prevent condensation forming during the winter lay-up.

- Plastic piping should never be used anywhere in the fuel system.

- Never try and bend an injector pipe – it will either kink or snap.

4
LUBRICATION

If an engine is to give long and reliable service it must be provided with clean oil of the correct grade and type for the service and conditions under which it is to operate.

Oil is very much more than a simple lubricant when used in a marine diesel engine as it must not only provide effective lubrication when the engine is running, but must also act as a cleaning agent carrying away harmful oxide deposits. Two other very important functions of the lubricating oil are its role as a cooling medium, carrying away heat from high temperature areas within the engine itself, and its ability to provide a degree of protection from corrosion when the engine is left standing idle during the season.

Modern oils include many additives which offer greater 'slipperiness' for improved lubrication and lower friction between moving parts plus anticorrosion inhibitors to coat the internal surfaces when the engine is idle. It is true to say that the more expensive the oil the higher the additive content and therefore the better the protection offered to the engine. Probably the most sophisticated oils generally available are those designed for turbo-charged engines which work under greater stresses than naturally aspirated (non-turbo-charged) units. They must also provide effective lubrication for the turbo-charger itself which may be running at anything up to 100,000rpm on high-performance engines! Although it is absolutely essential to use the correct grade of oil on turbo-charged engines it will equally benefit the naturally aspirated engine to use these top-quality grades.

The choice of whether or not to use a detergent oil depends on the type of engine, where it is operated and under what conditions. Detergent oils clean the engine and carry the products of combustion in suspension thereby preventing the build-up of oxidization on the internal surfaces. This is why a detergent oil will very quickly become blackened after an oil change as it rapidly collects the residue of the old oil remaining in the engine.

Modern oils designed for petrol engines are generally also suitable for non-turbo diesel engines and a quick check on the specification label on the can will confirm this. However, the use of non-detergent oils causes a gradual build-up of oxide within the engine. If a change is made to detergent oil after using non-detergent oil for a long period of time, it will usually be necessary to flush the engine through at least once to remove the excess combustion products which may be carried around in lumps within the engine after the initial change. The filter may require changing several times in a short period after the change-over. Once the detergent oil has done its work the oil-change periods can revert to normal practice.

The Lubrication System

The lubrication system is a fairly straight-forward arrangement, and apart from a general understanding of the way the oil is circulated and the work it performs on the way there is not a great deal to attend to in the matter of maintenance.

The oil is stored within a sump at the bottom of the engine below the crankcase or block. It is filled via the oil filler cap on top of the rocker or cam cover on the top of the engine. In some cases an additional filler is provided on the side of the sump for ease of topping up when the engine is tightly installed below the deck-head.

From the sump the oil is drawn up via a coarse strainer by the oil pump – this is

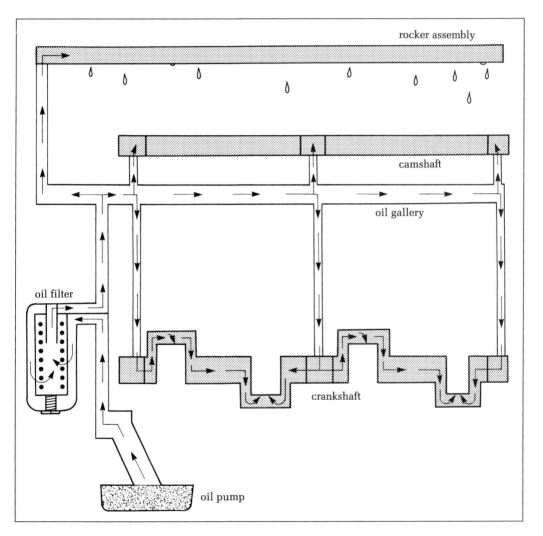

A simple schematic lubricating system for either two-stroke or four-stroke diesels.

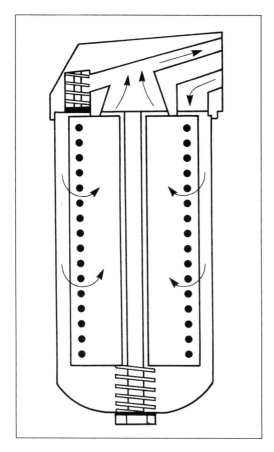

Cross-section of a typical paper-element-type oil filter with a relief valve which opens if the filter element becomes totally blocked.

the bearings takes the oil right around the journal and the bearing surfaces.

From the main bearings the oil is fed into drillings through the centre of the crankshaft to each individual big-end bearing. Depending on the engine design, the small-end bearings which are located at the top of the connecting rods are either fed with a supply of oil via a drilling through the connecting rod or via a spray system. In the latter case a drilling through the big-end lines up with the drilling in the crankshaft once every revolution and sprays oil under pressure up into the base of the piston where it flows on to the small-end bearing. Many high-powered engines, especially turbo-charged models, have additional piston cooling arrangements whereby oil is sprayed up under the piston crown. Here it may enter passages within the crown to circulate for maximum cooling effect before draining out and back into the sump.

Oil is also fed either directly from the gallery or the main bearings into the camshaft bearings via drillings in the block. Finally it arrives at the head and the valve rocker assembly where it drains back via the timing gears into the sump to be picked up again, cleaned within the filter and recirculated.

Turbo-charged engines generally utilize oil directly from the clean side of the filter via a pipe direct to the turbo-charger bearings which are lubricated and cooled before the oil drains back into the sump.

generally of the gear type driven from the timing gears at the front of the engine. The oil pressure relief valve is nowadays generally incorporated in the pump and therefore is beyond the attention of day-to-day maintenance.

From the pump the oil, now under pressure passes to the oil filter – often via an oil cooler – where it is cleaned of impurities and ready to be circulated around the engine. It then passes into the oil gallery where it is fed to the crankshaft main bearings. A channel in the face of

Maintenance

The two most important items of regular maintenance for the DIY owner are the regular changing of the engine oil and filter. If these slightly unpleasant tasks are performed at the intervals laid down in the manufacturer's instructions and the correct grade of engine oil is used, the life of the engine will be greatly enhanced compared with one which is neglected. The old saying that pleasure-boat engines corrode away before they can wear out can also be more or less discounted with the use of high-quality oils incorporating corrosion inhibitors

Changing the Oil

Changing the oil is a messy business at the best of times, and to avoid spreading spilt oil everywhere it is worth while spreading copious amounts of old newspaper all around the working area and under the engine itself. Before beginning the engine should be run to thoroughly warm the oil so that it will flow freely when draining.

If the engine is mounted high enough to allow the use of a drain tray beneath the sump the oil may be drained in the conventional manner via the sump drain plug. Before beginning the job ensure that there is sufficient room to get the full drain tray out from under the engine without having to tilt it! The majority of installations will have insufficient clearance for a drain tray and the oil will therefore have to be pumped out. Many engine manufacturers incorporate a sump pump in their standard engine specification. This means that all that is required is to operate the pump by hand to remove the oil which can then be pumped straight into an old oil can.

For engines without a built-in pump there are several hand- and electrically-operated pumps available which are supplied with special small bore tubes to

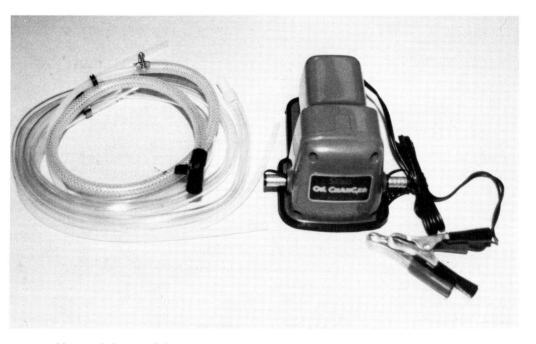

A reasonably priced electric oil changer pump.

fit down the dip-stick hole. I use an electric model which works very well and drains an 18-litre (4-gallon) sump in about two minutes.

Once the oil is drained the sump plug should immediately be replaced and tightened, and the engine can then be topped up with the new oil. The engine manufacturer's specification will usually include the oil capacity for a simple oil change as well as the additional capacity when the filter is changed. As the filter should always be changed on a marine engine when the oil is changed the latter capacity is the one to take note of.

Whether the oil is replaced before or after the filter is changed is really immaterial as the new oil will be unable to enter the filter until the engine is run. However, many owners prefer to drain the old oil and change the filter before topping up with fresh oil.

Changing the Oil Filter

Changing the filter on a modern engine is simplicity itself as spin-on filters are now the standard fitting. Spin-on filters are easily distinguishable from paper-element filters as they consist simply of a plain canister, usually with the maker's name displayed on the side. The paper-element-type filter has a central securing bolt through the bottom of the filter case.

To remove a spin-on filter, all that is required is to unscrew it and discard the entire assembly. Unfortunately this is seldom quite as simple as that as they tend to be rather tightly fitted. If you cannot remove the filter by hand pressure you will need a proper filter remover. This is a chain and lever arrangement where the chain is wrapped around the canister and secured on to the lever. Pressure on the

lever causes the chain to grip the canister allowing plenty of leverage for unscrewing even the most stubborn filters. The cheaper alternative to buying a filter remover is to stab the canister body with a large screwdriver and use this to provide the necessary leverage for unscrewing. Once the old filter is removed the new one may be fitted after smearing a drop of clean oil on the integral seal at the top of the canister. The canister should then be screwed home as tightly as possible by hand pressure alone.

To change the older paper element filter slightly more care is required than with the spin-on type as there is a seal at the top which must be replaced when the filter is changed.

The bolt at the bottom of the filter case is slackened with an appropriate sized spanner or socket until the case containing the filter element can be removed. For conventionally mounted filter bodies with the case hanging down, care should be taken to avoid dropping oil everywhere during this operation as the case and element holds around 0·5 litres (1 pint) of it. For filters which have been mounted upside-down the oil will have drained down and the problem will not arise.

Once the case is removed, the filter element can be extracted and discarded, being particularly careful to save any mounting washer which may have become stuck to the bottom of the element. This mounting washer sits on a spring in the bottom of the case and ensures that the filter element is securely held against the inlet and outlet oil ports within the filter head when assembled. Under the head of the filter assembly there is a recessed groove around the edge which locates the sealing washer which forms a seal with the lip of the case when reassembled. The

Stabbing a reluctant spin-on filter . . .

. . . for added leverage.

Smear the seal of the new filter with a drop of clean oil . . .

. . . before screwing home under hand pressure.

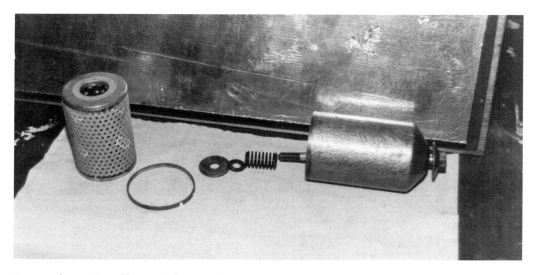

A paper-element-type filter ready for assembly.

sealing washer must be hooked out using a suitable implement such as a penknife blade or a small screwdriver. In many cases the new filter element will be provided with two or more new sealing washers to accommodate the filter arrangements of several different makes or models of engine, and it is therefore important to select the correct seal before reassembly by comparing the new seals with the old one. The correct seal may then be fitted into the recess in the filter head ensuring that it is sitting squarely within the recess and is not kinked or twisted. If it tends to drop out a small dab of grease will keep it in position.

The filter case should be cleaned out to remove all the old oil residue and any swarf which has congregated at the bottom. A wipe out with a clean paper towel is the most effective method. The new filter element can then be fitted on to the spring and washer within the base of the case and the entire assembly offered up under the filter head. The case may need to

be held up against spring pressure until the locating bolt is screwed home. Before finally tightening the bolt ensure that the lip of the case is evenly located within the recess around the head so that it compresses the seal to ensure an oil-tight joint. The bolt can then be finally 'snugged' up but not over-tightened.

Oil Leaks

The final maintenance item to consider within the field of the lubrication system is that of oil leaks. Minor oil leaks are little more than an annoyance and will not affect the performance or life of the engine, but major leaks could cause the engine to seize if they remain undetected, resulting in major damage.

To prevent an oil leak of this type causing major damage an audible warning of loss of oil pressure is worth arranging – a simple DIY audible alarm is demonstrated in Chapter 6. I have always used the simple audible warning device ever since a trip on my previous boat when a friend was at the helm. Being new to the boat he was not monitoring the instruments in the same manner that I, as a concerned owner, would do. While leaning on the cockpit coaming watching the world go by I had a strange sensation of impending doom which is now impossible to describe, but I strolled across the cockpit and casually looked at the instrument panel, only to find zero oil pressure on the port engine! I stopped the engine immediately and checked the engine compartment which I found smothered in oil which had sprayed out of a fractured gasket on the oil filter block. Happily my sixth sense had warned me in time to prevent the engine being damaged, but ever since that slightly eerie experience I have built in the low-cost audible warning system.

Happily, the majority of oil leaks are of the minor type and merely spoil an otherwise clean engine compartment if left unattended, so attention as soon as possible after they are discovered is recommended. Many leaks can be cured simply by tightening the securing bolts or nuts on whatever panel or casing the oil is escaping from. However, care is required not to over-tighten these as this will probably damage the gasket beyond repair by either crushing or splitting it. If the leak persists the only course of action is to replace the gasket with a new one.

When removing an old gasket it is essential to clean off every trace from the mating surface so that the new gasket has a perfectly smooth surface on which to form the seal. It is worth consulting the workshop manual before fitting a new gasket as some types of gasket are designed to expand when in contact with oil and are therefore best assembled without any gasket sealant being applied. The majority of cork gaskets will benefit from the application of a smear of gasket sealant of whichever type the owner prefers. With both surfaces clean, the gasket sealant is applied in a thin layer on to one face after which the gasket is fitted into place. The other face is then coated with sealant and the panel or casing is fitted into position. The securing nuts or bolts can be tightened lightly until all the surfaces are in contact, then after pausing for a few minutes to allow the solvents within the sealant to evaporate the job can finally be tightened, again ensuring that it is not over-tightened.

The rocker or cam cover gasket is often one which gives problems and is particularly annoying as any leaks from here will run right down the engine causing the maximum amount of mess. These gaskets are generally fitted dry to allow easy removal of the rocker/cam cover for periodical valve clearance adjustment. However, these gaskets have an annoying tendency to slip inside the cover as the bolts are being tightened. To prevent this happening I make a point of smearing one side of the gasket with sealant and then positioning it on to the face of the cover and leaving it until it has stuck in place. It is then possible to position the cover with care on to the engine and tighten the bolts without the gasket moving.

Probably the worst possible leak of a minor nature is that from the crankshaft rear oil seal. This seal is usually in the form of a graphite-impregnated rope quite similar in appearance to stern gland packing except that it is round in section while the packing is square. To replace this seal requires major dismantling of the engine and is almost certainly beyond the scope of the inexperienced owner. Leaks from this seal are generally minor and cause little more than a drip beneath the flywheel housing. A seal can often drip for years without giving any major problems although once the leak is detected it needs careful monitoring to ensure that it is not getting significantly worse. It should be attended to at the first convenient opportunity – usually at the end of the season when the boat is about to be laid up and therefore not interrupting the season's use of the boat. In fact, it would not do any harm to leave the leak for several seasons if it did not appear to be getting any worse – an oil-absorbent pad placed beneath the engine would keep the compartment clean.

SUMMARY

- Engine oil not only lubricates the moving parts, but also cleans the engine by carrying away dirt and grit in suspension.

- It also cools the hottest areas and offers a degree of anticorrosion protection during the winter lay-up period.

- The more expensive oils designed for highly stressed turbo-charged engines offer a greater range of additives to protect the engine in all conditions.

- Regular oil and filter changes help to ensure a long and trouble-free life for any engine.

- 'Spin-off' filters are easier and more convenient to change than the older canister style.

- Oil leaks should be attended to as soon as possible, although minor leaks may be left to the end of the season if they do not become any worse.

5
COOLING SYSTEMS

There are two possible cooling mediums available for marine engines – either water or air cooling. Air cooling is reserved for small engines which do not develop large amounts of power and is particularly popular on boats which use the inland waterways where weeds and rubbish can quickly block a water inlet strainer causing the engine to overheat. With air cooling all that is required is to provide an adequate supply of cool fresh air and the engine will run happily at a reasonable temperature.

It must be stressed that only engines designed and properly equipped for air cooling can be used as such as they generally incorporate ducting and finned flywheels to promote a rapid flow of air around the hot spots of the block. The size of the air intake vents makes it difficult to achieve a very quiet engine installation and the use of a dry exhaust also contributes to the noise. However, in areas of heavy water pollution the simple air-cooled engine has a lot to offer in terms of ease of maintenance and lack of corrosion.

The vast majority of engines nowadays are water cooled using heat exchangers or keel cooling which ensures that only fresh clean water circulates through the engine block. The advantage of this is that antifreeze and corrosion inhibitors can be added to the water for year-round engine protection.

Raw water cooling which takes the water straight out of the river or sea to circulate through the block is still used on certain engines. However, the corrosion and cold running problems which this system generates and which are covered in detail below are making it less attractive except where the very lowest initial costs are necessary.

Direct or Raw Water Cooling

The ultimate short-term money saver is the direct cooling system which takes raw water directly out of the sea or river, circulates it around the engine block, and finally discharges it overboard, usually via the exhaust pipework. There are, however, many drawbacks to this system. It is not possible to use a standard thermostat to allow the engine to run at its correct temperature of around 80–85°C (176–185°F) as this will eventually cause severe blockages to the water passages from impurities and silt building up on the walls.

The usual recommended working temperature for a direct-cooled engine is around 54°C (129°F) which causes some sludging of the oil as it can never achieve its optimum working temperature; the result of which is increased engine wear. The low temperature also means that items such as calorifiers for domestic

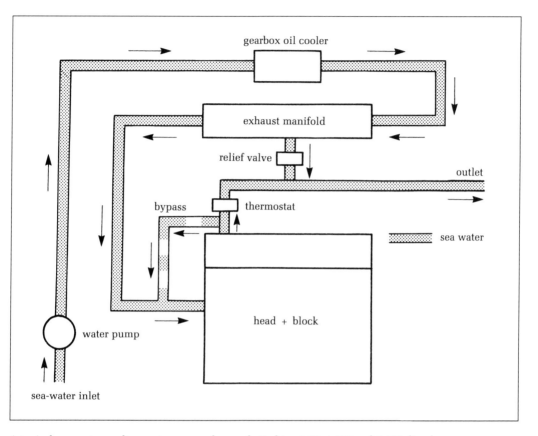

A typical raw water cooling system as used on early Perkins 4.99, 4.107 and 4.108 diesels.

water heating cannot be used effectively, but the last and most important point is that corrosion products from the hot raw water will continually attack the engine internals as it is impossible to add inhibitors to the water. The entire cooling system must also be drained during the winter months to prevent damage from freezing as antifreeze cannot be added.

Raw water cooling equipment will usually consist of an impeller-type water pump and water-cooled manifold plus a marine gearbox – either mechanical or hydraulic – and a gearbox oil cooler if required.

Indirect or Freshwater Cooling

None of the above-mentioned problems occur with indirectly cooled engines which have a separate freshwater supply within the engine block in the manner for which the engine was designed. This means that antifreeze and corrosion inhibitors can be added to the freshwater supply preventing the problems which beset raw-water-cooled engines. They can also use a standard thermostat and run at their correct designed temperature for maximum eficiency and long life, while

65

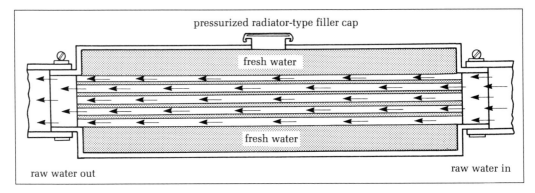

pressurized radiator-type filler cap

fresh water

fresh water

raw water out

raw water in

A heat exchanger – raw water enters at one end, passes through the tube stack and out at the other end. The fresh water enters near the top of the case and leaves near the bottom having been cooled while passing around the outside of the tubes. These inlets and outlets are positioned to suit the engine for which the heat exchanger is designed.

also supplying free hot water for the galley from a calorifier if required. The relatively modest extra cost is therefore well worth considering. Additional equipment required for indirect cooling includes a heat exchanger (often combined with the water-cooled manifold) and an engine oil cooler if required.

The Heat Exchanger

This piece of equipment (which on many engines is combined with the water-cooled exhaust manifold to make a neater installation) performs the same function as the radiator in a vehicle by cooling the water flowing around the engine block. With a radiator air forced through the matrix by either the forward motion of the car or the engine fan removes the excess heat, but with a heat exchanger raw water (drawn in from the sea or river by the raw water pump) removes the excess heat. It does this by circulating the fresh water (the water in the block) around a tightly packed tube stack in the heat-exchanger body. The raw water passes through the tubes and absorbs the heat before entering

the exhaust pipe and being discharged overboard back into the sea.

The tube stack is similar to that found in a steam engine boiler although the tubes in the heat exchanger are more tightly packed to give maximum cooling effect. The ends of the tube stack are sealed to prevent raw water mixing with the fresh making it possible to add antifreeze and anticorrosives to the system to keep the engine block in tiptop condition. It is important to have a reliable raw water inlet filter as the tubes can quickly become clogged if mud and weed are allowed to reach them. Part of the annual service should be to clean out the tubes by gently rodding through with a suitable piece of stiff wire such as a wire coat hanger.

For repair or replacement the complete stack is removable. The ends of the stack are revealed by removing the end covers from the heat exchanger, which will be either a neoprene type secured with jubilee clips or a metal plate with an O ring seal secured with bolts. Combined heat exchanger manifolds used on smaller engines directly replace the old exhaust manifold, while the larger single unit heat

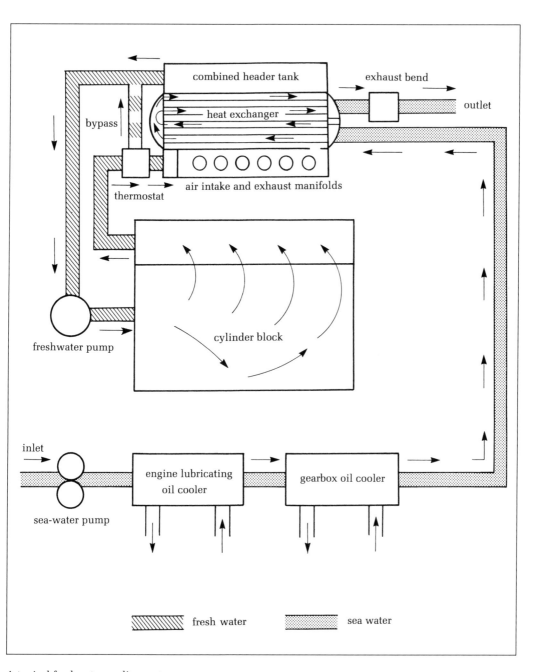

A typical freshwater cooling system.

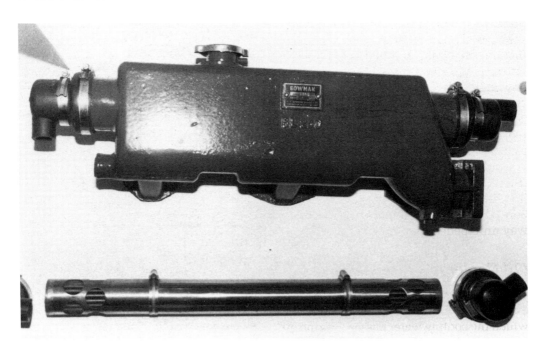

A combined heat exchanger/manifold with tube stack below.

exchanger usually bolts on to the front of the engine and may require additional support brackets.

Water-Cooled Exhaust Manifolds

Vehicle exhausts are cooled by air but as anyone who has accidentally touched one after a run will know they still become extremely hot! Without the air's cooling influence they would be quite capable of starting a fire, hence the need for water cooling in marine installations. The manifold itself is fairly simple in construction, consisting of a water jacket surrounding an internal tube manifold which keeps the temperature down to acceptable levels where there is no fire risk. It is possible to fabricate a manifold at home using only basic welding skills, although care must be exercised when aligning the mounting flanges for fitting to the engine otherwise exhaust leaks will occur. As these manifolds are not particularly expensive to buy it may not be worth the time and trouble to make one. Combined heat exchanger manifolds are very much more precise and are beyond the skills of the DIY enthusiast due to the intricacy of the tube stack.

The water-cooled manifold is a direct replacement for the original exhaust manifold and bolts straight into place. On engines where both the inlet and exhaust manifolds are on the same side it is often necessary to remove the inlet manifold and refit it upside-down to give clearance for the exhaust manifold to fit. Two older engines which immediately spring to mind are the BMC/BL 1.5/1.8 and 2.2/2.5-litre diesels. On other engines a replacement marine inlet manifold is required. It is feasible to run a diesel engine without any inlet manifold at all, although it is certainly not recommended. It would cause a great deal of induction roar – a requirement of most manifolds is to reduce this noise – and more importantly it would be impossible to arrange an air filtering arrangement which would inevitably lead to rapid wear of the engine bores due to the amount of dust finding its way unimpeded into the engine.

Oil Cooler

This is a smaller version of the heat exchanger with a tube stack through which the cooling water passes. Engine oil taken via a special adaptor (usually at the oil filter block) is pumped around the tubes and cooled. There are fewer tubes in the oil cooler as the oil does not require the same degree of cooling as the circulating water in the heat exchanger; indeed, if the oil is overcooled the problem of sludging and reduced lubricating efficiency can occur.

Raw Water Pump

These are almost universally of the flexible impeller type being very reliable and powerful for their size. As the name implies they are fitted on the raw water system and are in addition to the standard engine circulating pump on the fresh-water system. They are used to draw in cooling water from the river or sea for heat exchanger, exhaust manifold and oil cooling purposes.

'Jabsco' is the most famous name for this type of pump and has in fact become the

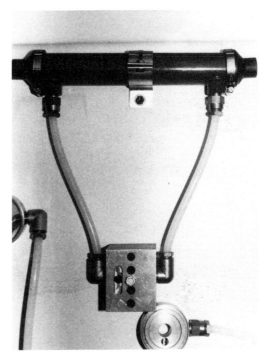

An oil cooler with adaptor for connecting to an oil filter block.

generic term for flexible impeller pumps in the same way that Hoover is the standard name for vacuum cleaners. There is a wide range of pump types to suit all engines in the marine leisure and light commercial field. Older types and those for slow-revving engines used plain bearings with greasers and adjustable glands, but the majority in service today use roller bearings which are lubricated for life, thereby cutting down on maintenance.

Several different drive methods are available, the simplest of which are fitted with a pulley and driven from an additional pulley on the front of the engine crankshaft pulley. The pump is simply mounted on a bracket which is bolted to the engine. Other types drive from a take-

A selection of Jabsco pumps for engine cooling and bilge pumping.

off in the engine timing case and are mounted directly on the engine in place of a blanking plate or some other piece of equipment such as a brake compressor which is not required on the marine version of the engine. For certain applications, high-speed types drive directly from the engine circulating water pump pulley. With this type the pump body is prevented from spinning by fitting a torque arm. This must be designed carefully so that it does not apply any side loadings on the pump bearing which would otherwise lead to premature bearing failure.

Whatever the drive type, all use neoprene impellers to pump the water so care must be exercised to ensure that they never run dry as this leads to rapid pump failure in a matter of minutes. For this reason it is a sensible practice to keep a spare impeller on board. It is also good practice to remove the impeller when laying up at the end of the season to prevent it freezing into place or permanently distorting. The direction of flow of the pump depends on engine rotation and is usually marked on the front cover plate of the pump. This should be noted when planning the pipework layout.

Keel and Tank Cooling

Keel cooling was quite popular a few years ago but is seen less often nowadays. By running heavy cooling pipes along the outside of the bottom of the hull, the engine circulating water is cooled by the flow of river or sea water passing around the pipes. This system is particularly useful in waters which suffer from excessive rubbish pollution as there is no intake filter to get blocked. A dry exhaust system is necessary unless provision is made to

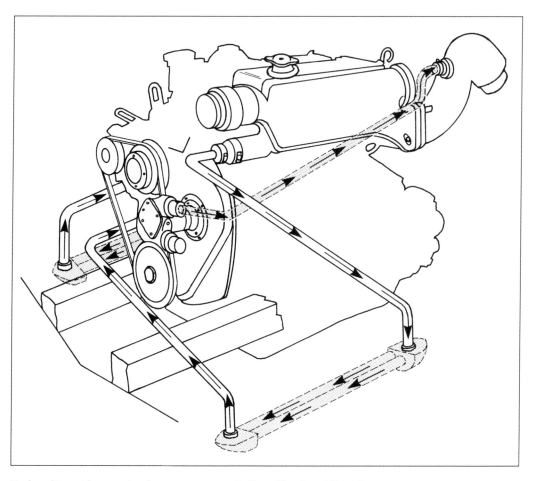

Keel cooling with an optional raw water pump indicated by dotted lines for a
water-cooled exhaust.

draw in water just for exhaust cooling, but this means the problem of rubbish blocking the filter is still present. The main problem is that the outside pipework is prone to damage from hitting underwater obstructions, thus requiring the boat to be slipped for repair.

Tank cooling is occasionally used on steel boats where a false bottom is welded into the bilge through which engine cooling water is circulated. It is cooled by heat transference through the bottom of the boat into the water outside. The same considerations for cooling the exhaust are required as for keel cooling, but the problem of damage to underwater pipework is removed. A large tank area is needed to make the system work efficiently but is suited ideally to the needs of narrowboat owners on inland waterways. It is sometimes possible to simply utilize the natural water flow and the engine

71

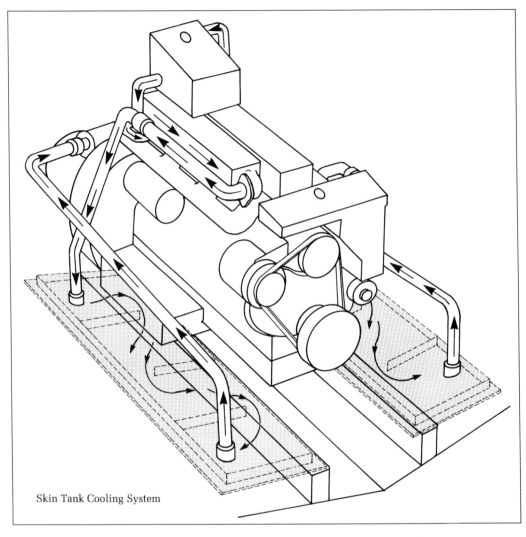

Skin Tank Cooling System

Tank cooling can work successfully although a large area of the tank in contact with the river water is essential if efficient cooling is to be obtained.

circulating pump to circulate the water in a tank cooling system, but if the bilge and tank are far below the level of the engine an additional flexible impeller pump will be required to ensure satisfactory flow.

The problem of whether to have a water-cooled exhaust also arises with this system as there is not a water intake in the same way as with a raw water or heat exchanger cooled system. A dry exhaust will tend to be more noisy than a water-cooled type and will also need to be carefully lagged to prevent the high temperatures within the pipe scorching or igniting surrounding timbers, or injuring unsuspecting crew members. However, the system is simplified without the need for a water inlet which a water-cooled exhaust will require. With a water-cooled exhaust the problems mentioned with the dry system do not occur although it is essential to arrange a warning system for overheating. If there is no warning system a blockage in the water inlet could go unnoticed until the exhaust became dangerously hot and, in the case of rubber exhaust hose which may melt in extremes of temperature, this could cause flooding of the boat.

The Jabsco Flexible Impeller Pump

One of the main advantages of the Jabsco impeller pump apart from its high pumping capacity is its ability to pass small solids without damage while successfully resisting excessive wear in sandy or gritty waters. Naturally the amount of abrasive material in the water will affect pump life but in all cases maintenance and repair can be carried out by unskilled DIY boat enthusiasts without the need for specialized knowledge or equipment. The comprehensive range of spares and impeller kits makes the boat owner totally self-sufficient when away from his home port, and this is an important consideration when cruising for long distances.

When selecting a pump for a particular engine which is not already catered for in the standard Jabsco engines list (this covers literally hundreds of engine models), the rule of thumb gives a water output at maximum engine revs and load for a diesel engine of $3 \cdot 2 - 3 \cdot 5 m^3/h$ of raw water when heat exchanger cooling is used. However, where a separate water-cooled exhaust manifold is used these figures are increased by a further $10-15$ per cent. The Jabsco pump catalogue which lists all the current engines for which standard pumps are available also contains an informative section on correct pump installation practice to avoid premature failure, especially of bearings, which can occur with either belt- or shaft-driven pumps.

The most common cause of shaft-driven pump failure is misalignment of the shaft which should be aligned in the same manner and with the same care as the vessel's propeller shaft. With the belt-driven pumps there are two particular problems to guard against during installation. The first is misalignment of the pulleys which will result in rapid belt wear and consequently early breakage. The second is over-tightening of the belt which will lead to premature bearing failure due to the unacceptably high side-loading placed on the pulley. Flange mounting pumps are gear driven and are probably the most reliable as they do not require the careful alignment of shaft drives or the regular belt tension adjustment of belt drives.

Finally, there is a choice of shaft seal depending on the pump model chosen. The simplest is the traditional gland packing used on pumps with plain bearings and which is not now generally used on modern marine engines as the gland needs to drip slightly to keep the packing moist.

The lip seal and mechanical seal are the most common types used on marine engines and both have their advantages. The mechanical seal consists of a carbon ring rotating against a stationary ceramic seat and has the advantage that it never wears the pump shaft. However, these types of seal are more critical to assemble and can cause problems for the amateur working on his or her own boat without suitable assembly tools. The lip seal with which many people are familiar in other applications is straightforward to assemble on to the pump but causes gradual shaft wear. However, most pumps incorporate a small spacer which can be removed when shaft wear is detected. This allows a new seal to be positioned further into the pump on an unworn portion of shaft thereby doubling the life of the shaft.

Pump Servicing

General Guidelines for All Pumps

When servicing pumps the cover plate is first removed by evenly slackening the fixing screws followed by the gasket – this will almost certainly tear as the cover is removed. The impeller should be removed next using either water pump pliers or two metal rods with rounded ends to gently lever the impeller up the shaft a few millimetres at a time. Screwdrivers should not be used as they will cut into the impeller hub causing irreparable damage.

The cam is removed next by slackening the securing screw. The cam may be stuck in place with gasket sealant but should pull away with very little pressure. Do not try levering it away as the edge may be damaged. There is a wear plate fitted into larger pumps and this can be removed once the cam is taken out.

Evenly slacken the cover-plate fixing screws.

Carefully prise out the impeller.

Remove the cam by slackening the securing screw.

High-Speed Pumps

The 22770 pump used in the photographs on pages 76 and 77 has a mechanical water seal which requires more care to replace than a lip seal. To replace the mechanical seal, the circlip which secures the bearing housing must be removed and is accessible through the cut-aways in the rear of the bearing housing. Once removed the bearing housing may be tapped lightly with a soft-faced mallet to separate the bearing, housing, shaft and ceramic (stationary) half of the mechanical seal from the pump body. The ceramic half of the seal can then be lifted off. On the larger 22740 high-speed pump the bearing is a press fit on to the spigot on the pump body and must be pressed off rather than tapped.

The carbon face half of the seal is tapped out of the pump body and discarded as it will be damaged during removal. The pump is now completely dismantled and may be cleaned of any corrosion before reassembly begins. If it is necessary to renew the bearing, the housing should slowly be heated in an oven until the bearing can be tapped out *gently*. It should never be pressed out as the housing is shrunk on to the bearing during initial assembly and will be damaged. When renewing a bearing in this way it is possible that the housing will become distorted, it is therefore simpler to order a new bearing and housing assembly complete.

Dismantling the 22770 pump. (a) Remove the circlip.

(b) Lift off the ceramic half of the seal.

(d) The pump is ready for cleaning and reassembly.

Reassembly of the pump is a reversal of the dismantling procedure and begins with the renewal of the carbon face half of the mechanical seal which should be a snug push fit within the pump body. Final location of the seal half must be made with

(c) Tap out and discard the carbon half of the seal.

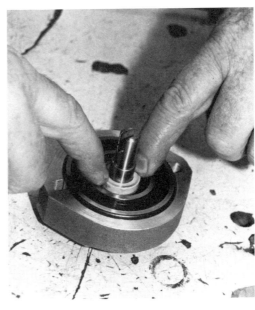

Reassembling the 22770 pump. (a) Carefully fit the carbon face half of the new seal.

(b) Next fit the ceramic half.

(c) Coat the face of the cam with gasket sealant.

(d) Ensure that the impeller drive pin is centralized in the impeller.

either a smooth bottomed tube of suitable size used as a drift, or better still a press. This is where the amateur is likely to find problems as without a suitable tube the seal will almost certainly be damaged and fail to function.

The ceramic half of the seal is slid on to the shaft and the face smeared with a light oil to provide lubrication on initial start-up. The pump body and bearing housing can then be pushed together and the circlip refitted. Lightly tap the circlip with a screwdriver and hammer to ensure that it is located securely in the groove.

The cam is fitted next and a generous coat of gasket sealant on the face will prevent air being trapped beneath the cam and causing priming difficulties on initial start-up. Before finally tightening the cam screw, tap the edge of the cam lightly to ensure that it is a flush fit with the body, and that the screw is of the correct length and does not protrude above the cam face – if it does so the impeller will be severely damaged as soon as the engine is started.

When fitting a new pin-drive impeller such as is used with this pump it is important to ensure that the pin is screwed through the impeller with no protrusion at either end otherwise damage may occur.

Before installing the impeller the inside of the pump body and the impeller itself should be lightly greased to assist initial pump priming. If the cover plate shows signs of excessive wear it may be installed inside-out to ensure that the correct running tolerances are maintained. For the same reason it is important to refit the gasket. It is permissible to fabricate a new gasket from plain brown paper if a proper replacement is not available. Tighten the securing screws evenly, being careful not to over-tighten them as they will snap if overstressed.

Flange Mounted Pumps

The 29500 pump, used in the photographs on pages 79 and 80, includes a multi-blade impeller and uses two bearings separated by a spacer to give longer bearing life by spreading the loading over a wider area. The bearings are lubricated by engine oil as they are open to the engine timing cover and receive an oil supply from the timing gears supply.

The impeller is spline driven and a spline seal is fitted over the end of the spline to prevent sand or grit damaging the spline itself. This will lift off with the impeller during removal and must be refitted on reassembly. The cam is then removed. There is a wear plate fitted behind the impeller which is located on a lug to prevent it rotating and which can be lifted out once the impeller and cam are removed.

The shaft and bearing assembly should be pressed out towards the flange after which the lip seals can be tapped out. There are two seals in this type of pump – one is for engine oil and the other for water. The engine oil seal prevents the oil in the timing cover from escaping while lubricating the pump bearings, and the water seal prevents water leaking from the pump body. A 'slinger' is fitted between the seals. This is a very important safety feature as in the event of the water seal leaking it throws the water outwards and prevents it from running along the shaft and creeping under the bearing oil seal from the non-pressure side – this would damage the bearings and contaminate the engine oil. The pump is now dismantled and can be cleaned ready for reassembly.

The bearings are an interference fit on the shaft and to replace them they must be pressed off with the spacer and the new

Dismantling the 29500 pump. (a) Ensure the spline seal is fitted.

(b) Remove the wear plate.

(c) Tap out the lip seals.

bearings fitted using a tubular drift on the bearing centre journal.

Each seal is pressed lightly into place with the lip towards the pressure side. This means that the open side of the seal with the spring visible around the inner lip should be facing the impeller on the water seal and the bearings on the oil seal so that the seals are actually back to back.

The slinger is slipped into the opening between the two seals prior to refitting the shaft and bearing assembly which is pressed into position.

If the wear plate is found to have excessive wear it may be reversed in the same way as the cover plate. Once this is replaced reassembly is exactly the same as described for the high-speed pump.

Although it has only been possible to cover the repair of two particular pump models, between the two, the details are

(d) The pump can now be cleaned and reassembled.

Always carry the correct spares kit.

similar for all other pumps in the Jabsco range and are also more or less similar for pumps from other manufacturers. There are service kits available for every pump and it is obviously essential to include the appropriate kit as part of the on-board spares store.

Winter Protection

It is during the winter months that the most extensive (and expensive) damage takes place on board craft which are left unattended. And it is often the engine which suffers the greatest, however, with a few simple and timely precautions all these problems can be avoided. The most obvious precaution to take is filling the freshwater cooling system with a good quality antifreeze. The best kinds are those which can be left in the system all year round and which offer corrosion protection as well as antifreeze properties. If this is changed once a year at the end of the season when the oil is changed it will help to keep the engine in tiptop condition throughout the year. Naturally this can only be achieved with freshwater-cooled engines although it is possible to introduce antifreeze into a raw-water-cooled engine's system by closing the water outlet hose connections, pouring in the antifreeze solution and closing the inlet. This will certainly be more beneficial than simply draining the engine down and leaving it dry.

If antifreeze is not used in a raw-water-cooled engine it must be drained down before leaving it for the winter. Boats with raw-water-cooled engines used on rivers and canals are particularly at risk from freezing damage as freshwater freezes at a higher temperature than salt water.

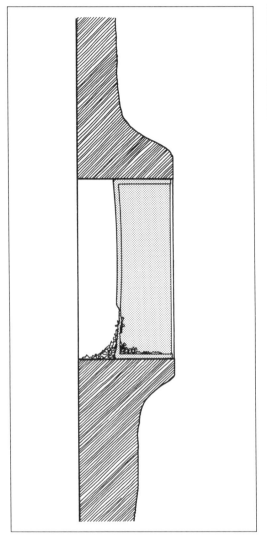

Cross-section of an expansion plug where silt
build-up inside has caused corrosion
and perforation.

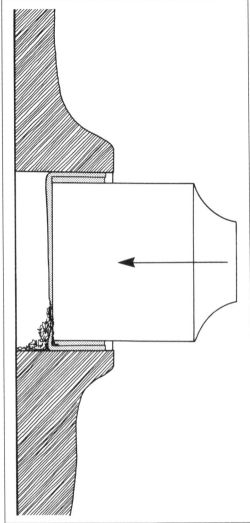

Replacing an old plug. (a) The old plug is tapped
lightly inwards to break the seal; an old damaged
socket spanner is an ideal tool.

Should the worst happen and the engine freeze solid it is to be hoped that the built-in expansion plugs (or core plugs as they are sometimes known) will do their job and pop out as the freezing water expands into ice. This is what they are designed to do, but in very severe conditions the rate of freezing may be too great to allow even expansion of the ice and the result will be a cracked block. If the block can be

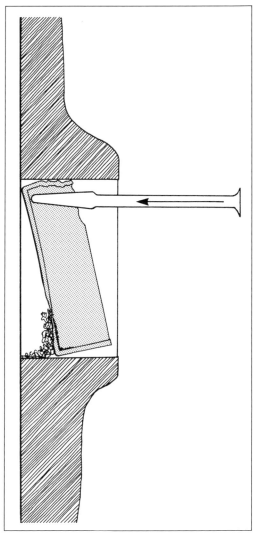

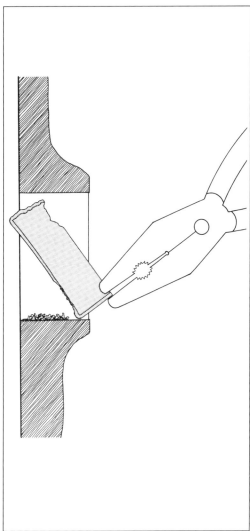

(b) It is then tapped on one side using a blunt cold chisel or similar tool to turn it sideways.

(c) Finally it is pulled out with the pliers.

repaired at all the engine must be removed from the boat and totally stripped down for welding. This is an expensive and time-consuming task which can easily be avoided by early precautionary measures.

From the foregoing it is easy to understand the important role which the humble expansion plug performs. Unfortunately, the light construction of these plugs makes them a prime target for corrosion and in time they will eventually begin to leak, at which point they should be replaced. This is normally a straightforward job except where the plug is

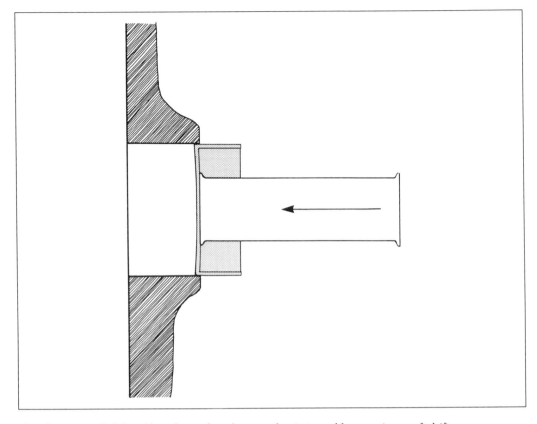

(d) After coating lightly with gasket sealant the new plug is tapped home using a soft drift in the centre of the plug.

situated in an inaccessible position such as behind the flywheel. In this case the gearbox will need to be removed, followed by the flywheel housing and flywheel before replacement can take place. In this case a temporary repair can often be achieved by using one of the leak remedies which are poured into the cooling system and which plug the gap from the inside.

Happily, the rest of the plugs are more accessible and replacement does not take long. Each plug is in the form of a dished cup and is an interference fit in its bore. The plugs are generally in stock sizes and can be bought in sets from most car accessory shops. To remove the old plug it should be tapped lightly inwards to break the seal of corrosion and sediment deposits which will have built up over a long period. Care must be taken to ensure that the plug is not tapped right into the block or an interesting half-hour will be spent trying to fish it out again. Once it has begun to move it can be tapped on one side to turn it sideways in its bore at which point it will be possible to either hook it out with the end of a screwdriver or pull it out using pliers or a vice-grip wrench. You should never attempt to prise it out against the face of the bore as this will damage the seal surface between the plug and the block and may lead to further leaks.

Once the plug has been removed the bore may be cleaned lightly using fine emery cloth to remove all the old sediment residue. The new plug should be smeared lightly with gasket cement around the outside of the sealing surface and then tapped lightly into position using a soft drift in the centre of the plug so that the convex surface causes a slight expansion of the seal surface as it is tapped home, thus making an effective seal. When the plug is located properly the seal surface should be flush with the face of the bore in the block.

Should the new plug show tendencies to weeping after fitting this will usually stop after a few hours. However, if it does not, the use of one of the proprietary cooling system conditioners will cure it and also assist with future corrosion prevention at the same time – these conditioners are therefore a worthwhile part of the cooling system annual service anyway.

SUMMARY

- The two main types of water cooling for marine engines are direct, where raw water from the river or sea is passed through the engine block, and indirect, where the raw water is passed through a heat exchanger which cools the fresh water circulating within the block.

- The advantages of indirect cooling are many and include the ability to use antifreeze and anticorrosion additives in the water system. The engine can run at its designed temperature for maximum efficiency while providing free domestic hot water from a calorifier if required.

- Apart from initial cheapness there are no advantages to direct cooling.

- Raw water pumps can be serviced by the DIY owner using ordinary tools and a service kit available world-wide from dealers.

- Expansion plugs should be examined for leakage due to corrosion and if found to be defective, replaced as soon as possible.

6
ELECTRICAL
SYSTEMS

Electrical systems and water, especially salt water, are poor companions, which means that the electrics on marine diesels need special care if they are to perform their duties in a safe and reliable manner.

Good installation practice is the first step towards a reliable system and this, coupled with regular simple maintenance, makes the difference between trouble-free cruising and endless problems.

Batteries

The heart of a boat's electrical system is the battery or batteries, and without these all but the smallest of engines cannot be started. Ideally batteries should be mounted away from the engine compartment in a separate ventilated compartment. However, it is usually more convenient to mount them within the engine compartment where leads to starter motors can be as short as possible to provide maximum current for starting with minimal voltage drop.

Batteries must be mounted securely, and a GRP box is an ideal housing for batteries as the resin is unaffected by acid. A plywood box glassed inside with two layers of chopped strand mat and resin is simple to make and provides a secure

home for the batteries when bolted down in a suitably ventilated compartment. It is possible to buy plastic battery boxes from chandlers which are also immune to acid and which incorporate a lid, but these are not available in sizes to suit large batteries and anywhere are not strong enough to give adequate support to the batteries in rough weather.

Not only must the battery box be strong but the batteries must also be fixed firmly within the box to prevent them moving about. This can be achieved by providing a lip on the bottom of the box for each battery to sit in and then bolting a timber strap across the top of the batteries. A lid is an important item which should be included in home-built battery boxes as it prevents metal items such as spanners falling on top of the batteries and causing a massive short circuit which would be followed by a fire, or an explosion in a shower of acid.

It is important to arrange an efficient ventilation system for batteries mounted in the engine compartment as they gave off relatively large quantities of hydrogen under conditions of heavy charging. This can lead to an explosion if contact is made with sparks from unprotected electric motors. It is therefore essential to ensure that all ventilation extractor fans are of

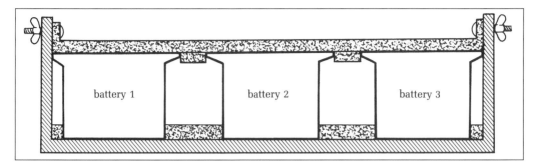

Cross-section of a battery box with firm battery support.

the sealed sparkproof type. For the same reason, all electrical equipment should be switched off every time before the battery terminals are disconnected. If you do not

Batteries secured in a strong GRP-lined box with sparkproof extractor fan directly overhead.

do this the small arc as the terminals are lifted could similarly cause an explosion with quite catastrophic results for the person next to the batteries!

It is important to ensure that the battery for engine starting is of more than adequate capacity for the size of engine. It will ideally be of a greater capacity than the battery used for starting the vehicular equivalent of the boat's engine. This allows for a certain amount of self-discharge should the boat be left unused for a long period.

All the terminal connections on batteries and isolating switches should be clean and kept greased with either vaseline or one of the proprietary battery terminal greases available from motor accessory shops. Battery electrolyte levels should be checked as part of the weekly engine service schedule of oil and water levels, topping up as necessary using de-ionized water. Any sudden drop in electrolyte level will indicate a damaged battery casing or possibly severe over-charging causing buckled plates in the battery and irrevocable damage. Modern low-maintenance batteries should not require topping up more than about once a year, but if an over-charge situation arises, even these will need more frequent attention – a clear indication that the entire system needs checking. Maintenance-free batteries (which are of course more expensive) can almost be fitted and forgotten but even these need to have their terminals cleaned and greased occasionally.

Batteries deteriorate most rapidly when the boat is laid up throughout the winter and they are left in a discharged state – they may even freeze and split the casing. The best way to treat the batteries is to charge them fully at the end of the season and then give them a trickle charge top-up every month throughout the lay-up period. If it is not possible to get down to the boat regularly it is best to take the batteries home where they can be properly cared for.

Battery Isolating Switches

Cut-out switches to completely isolate the battery from the electrical system should be heavy enough to carry all the current demands for the craft, including starting current. Models are available to fit directly on to the battery terminal posts or for remote mounting. The latter type can be obtained in models for switching in two batteries, either separately or in parallel pairs. The drawback with this type is that longer battery leads are required, travelling from battery to master switch and then to the starter motor via the solenoid. Over very long runs this can lead to voltage drop causing starting problems, especially in very cold weather when the

A heavy-duty battery isolating switch capable of handling starting current of 1,000 amps for ten seconds.

A Bosch 12-volt 90-amp alternator with twin-belt drive.

engine oil is particularly viscous. Care is therefore required in the siting of cut-out switches to keep cable runs to a minimum. Remotely switchable isolating switches are available which solve the problem of long cable runs as the main current-carrying switch can be mounted near the batteries while the operating switch is mounted in any convenient position within the boat.

As battery power increases it becomes necessary to fit larger alternators to provide adequate charge for this increased capacity. It is quite common to have two alternators fitted to an engine. This simplifies the circuitry to some extent as the starting and domestic circuits can be run totally isolated from one another with

just an emergency cross-over switch should the starting batteries fail. It also provides a simple means of having both 12- and 24-volt systems on board if this is required.

Specialist marine electronics companies are able to advise on battery/alternator matching. Motor vehicle alternators perform perfectly adequately in a boat if protected from water and given an occasional spray with a water-repellent to prevent corrosion. As cars have become more sophisticated, large capacity vehicle alternators have become readily available at reasonable prices, whether new, reconditioned or second-hand from the local breaker's yard. In fact, the most economical method of obtaining a good spare alternator is to buy one second-hand at the breaker's and then use it as an exchange for a reconditioned unit. This will almost always work out more economical than paying the surcharge for buying a reconditioned unit outright with no exchange.

If the engine relies solely on battery power for starting (as do all large capacity marine diesels in common use) then the two-battery system – one for engine starting, one for domestic use – is essential and not difficult to arrange. Ideally, the two-battery system utilizes a blocking diode arrangement between the alternator and batteries, but unless the alternator is of the battery-sensed type the diode will prevent adequate charging due to the loss of approximately 1 volt through the diode. The standard alternator charging voltage of approximately 14 volts is reduced to 13 volts by the time it reaches the battery, and this is insufficient to overcome the battery's own internal resistance

which increases as a full state of charge is approached.

Heavy-duty charge-splitting relays are another option for twin-battery systems, and as they do not affect charging voltage they are therefore suitable for use with machine-sensed alternators. These are often activated by a switch in the engine's oil pressure circuit which connects both batteries in parallel for charging as soon as the engine is running and separates the circuits when the engine stops. A simpler system operates when the ignition is switched on and the relay is energized directly from the key switch. A simple, manually-operated switch may replace the blocking diode or relay if preferred, but it is important to remember to swtich off when you stop to separate the battery systems, and to switch on again when running to charge both batteries.

Standard vehicle alternators are of the machine-sensed type as they are cheaper to produce and perform adequately for

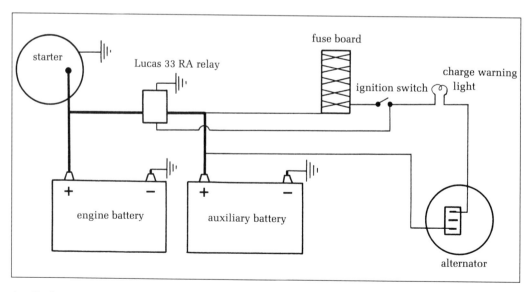

A split charge system using a Lucas relay.

vehicle duties. Machine sensing means that the regulator senses the state of the battery charge at the alternator rather than at the battery and cannot therefore compensate for losses within the wiring or through a blocking diode. The battery-sensing alternator senses the state of charge at the battery itself and can therefore compensate for any losses in the system and adjust the rate of charge accordingly to overcome these losses.

The simplest way to convert a standard ex-vehicle alternator from machine to battery sensing so as to utilize simple diode charge-splitting equipment is to fit one of the latest external electronic charging regulators. Not only does this convert the alternator from machine to battery sensing, it also increases the efficiency of the alternator, thereby ensuring that it is always supplying the needs of the battery under all conditions.

The latest advanced alternator controllers are more robust than some of the earlier versions. They utilize extra-robust components and are built with quality control to a high standard to ensure that some of the shortcomings of the earlier units are removed while still retaining all the excellent features which have made such an impact on battery-charging technology.

Alarm features which warn of problems within the system such as low state of charge or overvoltage are often included, as well as automatic temperature compensation which adjusts the rate of charge dependent on the ambient temperature within the battery compartment at any time. Being fairly straightforward to fit they are ideal for the DIY enthusiast with a limited knowledge of electronics and who wishes to improve his or her boat's charging performance and at the same time increase battery life.

We have already mentioned briefly the battery's internal resistance which with a standard alternator prevents the battery from ever reaching a full state of charge once it has become more than about 70 per cent discharged. This is due to the fact that the standard machine-sensed alternator never knows what is actually happening at the battery and it can therefore only provide a steady output of about 14 volts. The advanced alternator controller monitors the actual state of charge of the battery and adjusts the alternator output accordingly, raising the charging voltage to overcome internal resistance and bringing the battery back up to a full state of charge. It also compensates for diode charge splitters within the system by raising the voltage to overcome the 1 volt loss through the diode.

The most visible effect of fitting an electronic regulator, apart from all the advantages mentioned, is the speed with which batteries are re-charged. Most boat owners with ammeters on the instrument panel will have noticed how even with a heavily discharged battery the charge from a standard alternator starts at a high rate and very soon drops down to a trickle. This means that the battery takes a long time to re-charge, and in fact never reaches a full state of charge. With an advanced alternator controller controlling the same alternator the charge rate remains at a high rate to charge the battery quickly but without causing it to over-charge or gas excessively.

Instruments

Instruments for the engine vary greatly in price but these cannot generally be bought second-hand as the head and sender need

A standard Lucas 17ACR alternator converted to drive a tachometer via the cable protruding from the back of the case.

to be compatible. Car accessory shops are a good source of cheap instruments, but these will not be protected against the marine environment so a regular spray with a water repellent will be necessary to make sure of reliable performance and long life.

Tachometers for diesel engines also vary in price and drive type. The simplest is the cable-driven type but this cannot readily be adapted for dual-helm read-outs. They also require a drive take-off on the engine. Perception head types are easier to fit as most gearbox adaptor plates are now drilled to take them. Four shallow holes are drilled concentrically opposite each other in the face of the flywheel through the tapped hole in the adaptor plate. A magnetic sensor is then screwed into the hole leaving a gap of around $\frac{1}{32}$ in clearance between the face and flywheel and which senses the engine revolutions as the drilled holes pass its face. Being an electronic unit more than one read-out is available, thus making it suitable for twin-helm positions. Probably the most popular type of tachometer today receives its signals from the alternator via a tapping in the field windings. Many modern alternators already have a take-off for this purpose but if not, any auto electrician will make the necessary solder connection for a small fee. This type is also suitable for dual-helm applications.

Connections

Good connections are essential to a reliable electrical system, and every joint without exception should be made with either a soldered or crimped terminal. It can be tempting to twist a couple of wires together and bind them with insulating tape and the item will no doubt work quite satisfactorily, but by using this method a potential failure point and fire hazard is installed. Insulating tape does not last long in a hot and oily atmosphere and once it has dropped off, bare wires are left just waiting to short out and cause a fire, or simply corrode away and break the circuit.

Heavy starter cables must be of sufficient capacity and have properly fitted terminals if lively starter performance (and easy starting) is to be achieved. Clamp-type fittings are the most reliable for taper-post terminals and should be screwed and soldered to the cable. Ford-type block terminals require a heavy eyelet terminal which is crimped and soldered. This same type of eyelet should be used for connecting to master switches and starter motors. Various sizes of eyelet are available from motor and electrical shops and it is important to use the correct size for the job.

Nowadays, with the wide variety of crimped terminal kits readily available there is no excuse for making bad connections. At one time all connections would have been soldered, but a proper crimped connection is as reliable as a good soldered one and is very much better than a bad one. Crimp terminal kits usually include a cutting/crimping tool and a selection of terminals, including bullet connectors (male and female for in-line connections), spade connectors (also male and female, generally for equipment connections but also for in-line connections) and eyelets in various sizes, mainly for equipment connections which do not accept spades.

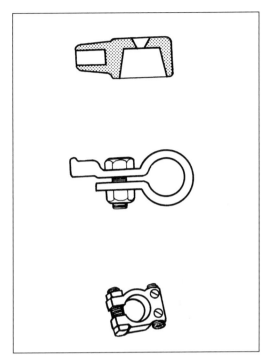

A selection of battery terminal connectors.

Each type of connector is available in three colour-coded sizes to suit different gauge cables. Red is for the smallest cable sizes, blue for medium sizes and yellow for larger cables. The crimp tool has three crimping sizes which are also colour coded to ensure that the correct crimping pressure is applied to each connector. This makes it possible for the DIY enthusiast to make professional-quality joints every time at minimal cost.

Finally, there are the plastic connecting strips which have many uses as cable junctions and even in-line connectors.

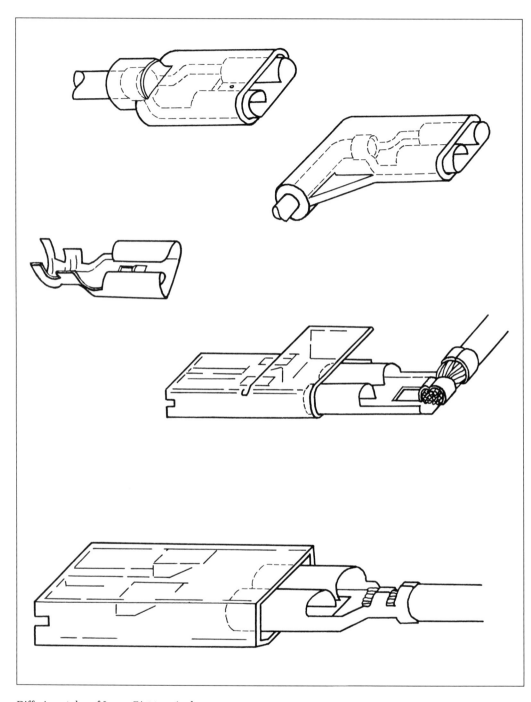

Differing styles of Lucas-Rist terminals.

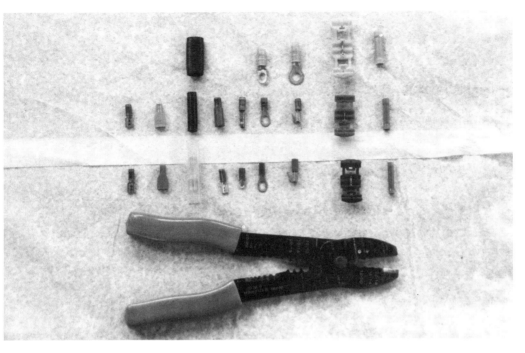

A selection of readily available connectors and crimping tool.

They are easy to use and infinitely preferable to the 'twist and insulate' joint mentioned earlier. This is a good item to have as part of your electrical spares kit and will always make a reliable if bulky joint.

Wiring

All cables whether for starting, charging or instrumentation must be of a size heavy enough to carry the maximum load required with a good safety margin to prevent overheating and possible insulation failure. Cable runs should be loomed neatly using either plastic spiral wrap or insulating tape. Once off the engine cables should be run in conduit to protect them from physical damage. An

Not the neatest of joints, but reliable and secure.

95

Cable Sizes and Capacities

Cable Sizes and Current-Carrying Capacity of PVC-insulated multi-strand cable

Cross-section in sq. mm	Amperage
1	8
1·5	12
2	16
2·5	19
3	27
4	31
6	42
10	70
25	170
50	345
70	485

neat and allows plenty of air to circulate around the loom. It is good practice to avoid running cables through the bilges wherever possible.

Additional Circuits

A useful addition where dual-battery systems are employed either with twin engines or a single engine and separate domestic battery is the facility to connect all batteries in parallel temporarily for engine starting should the main starting battery be discharged for any reason. This is simple to arrange by fitting remote starter solenoids between each battery connected with heavy starter cable of the same gauge as the main starter cable. Solenoids are available from car accessory shops at a reasonable cost, but it is essential to order one with the correct voltage of either 12 or 24 volts. If there are two batteries to be paralleled then only one solenoid is required. If three batteries are to be paralleled they will require two solenoids unless a selector switch is fitted between two of the batteries which can

added advantage of conduit is that when extra circuits are required it is possible to feed additional wires through the conduit without disturbing the surrounding equipment and fittings.

Complex wiring such as that behind the instrument panel should be laid out neatly and can be loomed conveniently using plastic spiral wrap. This keeps the wiring

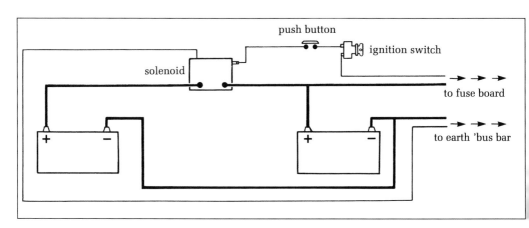

A simple circuit for placing batteries in parallel when the starter battery is run down.

select both and which therefore takes the place of one solenoid.

The solenoid must be mounted securely near the batteries and the body of the solenoid, if a vehicle type, must be earthed to the batteries' negative earth board otherwise it will not operate. The other connections are simple with the two large terminals taking the heavy cables from each battery positive terminal and the single small connector (usually of the spade type) taking the cable from the operating button. A press button is ideal for the purpose as it ensures that the batteries cannot inadvertently be left connected in parallel which would dras-

tically shorten the solenoid life. A button designed for 12 and 24 volt DC use is essential for operating the solenoid due to the relatively high current draw when the solenoid throws in. The feed to the button ideally is taken from the ignition key switch so that it can only be used when the ignition is switched on.

To operate the system if the engine battery is too low to turn the engine fast enough to start, all that is required is to hold the button in while turning the engine over and release it as soon as it starts. With all the boat's batteries in parallel the engine should spin over very fast and achieve a quick start.

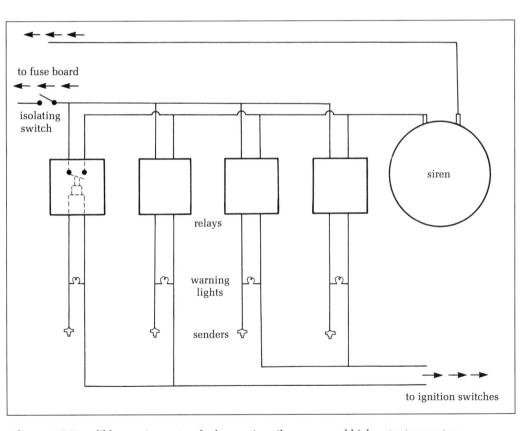

A low-cost DIY audible warning system for low engine oil pressure and high water temperature.

Another useful DIY addition to the electrical system is an audible alarm monitor to warn of low engine oil pressure or high water temperature. This can operate from the warning lights of each circuit and thereby utilize the senders which are already fitted to the engine. This is particularly useful when an autopilot is used extensively and the instruments are not monitored continually or when an inexperienced helmsman is on duty. It is also a good safeguard against unauthorized meddling with the controls when in harbour as the siren will sound as soon as the ignition is switched on providing the isolating switch is in the 'on' position. In fact, the only time the isolating switch should be off is when the engines are first started so that the siren does not deafen everyone on board.

The parts required are accessory relays for each function – two relays for a single engine and four for twin engines – plus a high-pitched warning siren and an isolating switch. For engines without high temperature warning lights a low-cost sender is available from Lancing Marine which clamps to the water injection fitting on the exhaust manifold outlet and which gives early warning of raw water pump failure or a blocked water inlet strainer.

The relays can be mounted in any convenient and dry location near the instrument panel and close to the siren. Wiring is straightforward with a feed being supplied to the isolating switch from any convenient fused point. From the switch a connection is taken to one of the terminals on the function side of each relay. The connection from the other function terminals goes to the positive connection of the siren. The siren's negative connection goes to a convenient negative earthing point in the electrical system.

There are two connections to each warning light and these are extended to the two operating terminals on each relay with each light operating one relay. As soon as a light illuminates, the appropriate relay throws in and the siren operates. This simple safety device is fairly cheap, with all parts being readily available from the local car accessory shop.

Maintenance

Older types of dynamo had an oiling point on their back bearing housing which required a few drops of oil during service, but later types and alternators are now generally maintenance-free apart from the need for an occasional clean and spray with lubricating water repellent. Drive belts should be checked during engine service – dynamo belts require about 2·5cm (1in) of up-down movement on the longest straight section, while alternator belts need to be tighter with 1cm (0·5in) movement. A screeching sound after you first start the engine is a sure indication that the alternator belt is loose and requires either tightening or replacing.

The starter motor is generally installed at the lower end of the engine near the bilge, and should be checked to ensure that it is not swimming in oily bilge water. A good squirt of lubricating water repellent inside and out should keep it operating smoothly. (After using one of these sprays on any equipment allow about half an hour before operating, as the solvents in the spray are highly inflammable and will be ignited by sparks in the motor.)

Check the bilges as part of the laying-up routine performed at the end of the season to ensure that water is not lying beneath the engine and keeping the starter motor and alternator permanently damp. This should be sufficient to see them through the worst of the winter weather.

SUMMARY

- Good installation is the key to reliable electrical systems.

- Batteries should be securely fixed in boxes with fitted lids.

- Extractor fans in battery compartments should have spark-proof motors.

- Every circuit should be protected with a fuse or circuit breaker.

- Battery isolating switches must be capable of carrying full starter current.

- Twin battery split charge systems are essential to prevent the engine starting battery being inadvertently flattened by domestic use.

- Advanced alternator controllers allow battery sensing while ensuring that the battery always receives a full charge.

- Crimp terminal kits offer the DIY owner the opportunity to make professional quality joints at low cost.

7

TURBO-CHARGERS
AND AFTER-COOLERS

A simple method of increasing the power of diesel engines is to fit a turbo-charger. This gives a worthwhile increase with little effort and only moderate expense making it the ideal method for manufacturers to offer the same basic engine in a variety of power outputs to suit differing applications. The next step up the power boosting ladder is to fit an after-cooler (or inter-cooler) which again often requires no further work than basic fitting. After this it becomes necessary to rework the internals of the engine or to totally redesign the block at which stage costs begin to escalate rapidly.

To achieve diesel power-to-weight ratios approaching that of petrol engines the use of turbo-charging is now common practice. 'Turbo' has been the 'in' word with advertising executives for several years now, many of whom have probably no idea of the meaning of the word. It derives from 'turbine' which is the basis of the turbo-charger. A turbine with vanes driven by the exhaust gases and rotating at up to 100,000rpm is connected to a vane-type air pump which raises the pressure of the air entering the cylinders by amounts ranging from $0.63-2.1\text{kg/cm}^2$ (9–30 p.s.i.) depending on the engine and its proposed use. The increased pressure means that more air enters the cylinder

and this, coupled with a greater quantity of atomized fuel, means that extra effort is applied to the piston on the downward part of the combustion stroke, thus resulting in more power from the engine. A turbo-charger alone can increase the

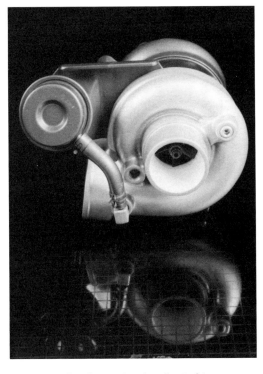

Compact turbo-charger fitted to the Perkins Prima marine diesel.

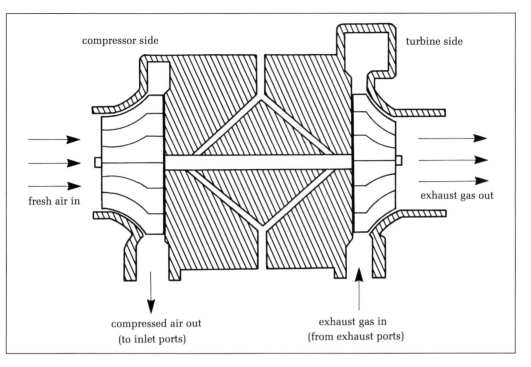

compressor side

turbine side

fresh air in

exhaust gas out

compressed air out
(to inlet ports)

exhaust gas in
(from exhaust ports)

Cross-section of a typical turbo-charger.

power of a standard engine by up to as much as 60 per cent depending on the pressure increase. However, as pressure is increased the temperature of the air increases causing expansion and therefore allowing a proportionately smaller amount of air to enter the cylinder – this means that a stage is eventually reached where the turbo-charger is defeating its own object.

At this stage a charge air-cooler is required if the power of the engine is to be further boosted. The charge air-cooler (also called an after-cooler or inter-cooler) cools the compressed air before it enters the cylinder. This causes the air to contract and thereby allows a greater amount of air to enter the cylinder. The extra air coupled with a greater amount of

atomized fuel gives the extra power output from the engine.

The charge air-cooler is similar in design to the normal heat exchanger used for engine water cooling with a tube stack around which the charge air flows while the cooling water passes through the tubes. To provide the most effective level of cooling, raw water is usually passed through the after-cooler immediately after leaving the water pump while it is still cold, and in this way it reduces the temperature of the induction air significantly.

Using a turbo-charger, charge air-cooler, modified pistons and fuel-injection equipment can increase the power of an engine by over 100 per cent, but it must be borne in mind that the pressures on the engine are high. This high pressure will cause greater wear and tear to the engine when it is used at full throttle so it is essential to match this with enhanced servicing and engine care – in other words, regular maintenance carried out at shorter intervals. Engine oil and filter changes are particularly important as the close tolerances of the turbo-charger require clean oil at all times. The correct grade of oil must also be used which will be of a higher grade than for unboosted engines.

For the express cruiser owner requiring ultimate power with diesel reliability a boosted diesel engine is the obvious choice giving the additional advantage of improved fuel economy power for power over unboosted engines due to the extra fuel efficiency of turbo-charged units. For the owner who must run his or her craft on a shoe-string budget with minimal maintenance, the unboosted engine is the better alternative as it will be less demanding in its servicing requirements. However, any engine whether boosted or not will reward its owner with long life and reliability if serviced at the correct intervals using high-quality oils and regular filter changes. In fact, other than ensuring a clean supply of the correct grade of oil there is no maintenance work for the DIY owner to undertake on his or her turbo-charger, which should be left to specialists when repair or overhaul is necessary.

SUMMARY

- Turbo-chargers offer a relatively low cost method of increasing power output.

- Inter-coolers (or after-coolers) take this one step further.

- Turbo-charging is now giving diesel engines power-to-weight ratios approaching that of petrol engines, with far greater fuel economy and safety.

8
MARINIZATION

Large engine manufacturers such as Perkins and Volvo convert their own engines and sell them directly as marine units. In this case the base engines are usually manufactured with subtle differences to make them more suitable for the marine field – for example, corrosion-resistant materials are used which would not normally be required for road or industrial use. Specialist marine conversion companies such as Mermaid and Sabre who both specialize in Ford engines must make such internal alterations once they get the base engine into their workshops. This does not make one type of engine any better than another as both the original manufacturer and the marinizer take great care in the preparation of their finished product.

Almost every engine manufacturer offering marine versions of their base units also supplies vehicle engines and each marine unit will have its counterpart in a vehicle. This means that spares from the local truck and van dealer will almost certainly be significantly cheaper than the 'marine' equivalent. A certain large engine manufacturer whose marine engine spares are legendary for their expense will deny that truck spares are suitable for marine engines, but when the two types of part are compared they are generally found to be identical.

Many DIY boat-building enthusiasts purchase second-hand engines from vehicle breakers' yards, and after re-conditioning them they convert them to marine use by buying the same or similar parts as are used by the professional marinizing companies. This is a very cost-effective method of obtaining power for a boat and at the end of the day all these engines are basically the same under the skin as their truck or van counterparts.

Marinizing an ex-vehicle engine for marine use is often regarded as a technical subject best left to experts and engineers, but for the DIY enthusiast with limited resources it is a very good way to save a lot of money when considering a replacement engine or when installing machinery in a new boat on a limited budget.

The true marine engine with its heavy build and very slow-revving performance designed exclusively for boat use no longer exists for the average small-boat owner. Instead, all the engines offered by the big names in the marine field are modified versions of light industrial, car and truck units. They are either converted to marine specification at the factory or taken in by the marinizing companies in basic standard form and modified for marine use with the fitting of suitable water cooling equipment – this is why so many companies offer the same basic makes of engine under differing brand names. Ford, Mitsubishi, Peugeot and more recently Vauxhall are just some of the makes of diesel engine currently being marinized by different specialist companies. In many cases the only work required to turn a vehicle engine into a perfectly serviceable boat power unit is the addition of the water cooling equipment. However, with the present demand for higher power outputs many companies also modify the basic engines internally to accommodate this need.

Choosing an Engine

The first and most important step is to choose a suitable engine. It is at this stage that the required performance of the boat must be decided upon, and it is this which will then give an indication of the size of engine and power output required to provide this speed. Many people are disappointed with the performance of their craft having fitted an engine which does not have sufficient power for their cruising aspirations. There are fairly simple formulae which will give a good indication of the power required for a given speed while companies like Lancing Marine can give specific advice on this area. There is not a great difference in cost between marinizing engines of different sizes when the engine is purchased on the second-hand market so it is worthwhile to err on the larger side if this is possible. Extra power does not have to be used but it is always there if required in an emergency.

Before making the final selection of engine make and model it is essential to check with the marinizing equipment supplier that marinizing equipment is readily available off the shelf for that particular engine. There is little point in doing the job to save money if the engine requires extensive modifications resulting in large bills for one-off engineering work just to enable the marinizing parts to fit. Perkins engines are a particular example of this as so many types of each model are produced; some are very expensive to marinize, requiring extensive modification and additional parts. Again, Lancing Marine are a good source of advice on this point.

The cheapest method of obtaining a basic engine is to buy from a local vehicle breaker's yard; of course there is always an element of risk when buying second-hand so it is advisable to have some idea of how to pick a good engine before buying. It is quite possible to pick up a low mileage engine in good condition requiring nothing more than a repaint prior to marinizing. One of these engines would usually come from a late model vehicle involved in an accident which has written off its body; although initially more expensive than a well-worn example, it can mean a worthwhile saving in preparation time.

A good commercial vehicle breaker's yard will be able to start up the chosen engine while it is standing on the ground. It is worthwhile explaining what the engine is for and whether it is for immediate use or for reconditioning, as the breaker will then be able to select a suitable unit of the make and model decided upon. A check of the exterior of the engine for broken or damaged parts can then be followed by a look inside the rocker cover. The condition of the oil on the surfaces of the rocker assembly will give a good indication of the engine's internal condition. On a diesel the oil should be jet black although if it is also very 'sludgy' this may indicate badly worn piston rings. If it is milky in colour this indicates water in the oil and unless it has obviously entered while the engine has been standing in the open it is advisable to reject this engine.

In the few minutes that the engine runs with the residue of fuel still in the system it is possible to get a further indication of its overall condition. If it bursts into life without hesitation and runs smoothly without undue smoke from the exhaust or obvious knocks and rattles, especially on the over-run and when ticking-over, then the indications are that it will be in fairly good condition. A burst of throttle to see how responsive the engine is will also indicate that the fuel pump governor is functioning properly. (Care is essential when doing this on a free-standing engine to ensure that the torque does not cause it to topple over!)

For anyone without the personal knowledge or knowledgeable friends to assist with picking a suitable engine, a good compromise is to buy a worn example of the engine required at a knock-down price, then use it to exchange for a reconditioned unit from one of the many specialists in the vehicle engine reconditioning field. In this way the end result is an engine which carries a guarantee and which is ready for marinizing at a fraction of the price of a new unit. If this course of action is chosen it is essential to ensure that the engine chosen is suitable for reconditioning with no broken parts, otherwise the reconditioner will not accept it in exchange.

Preparation

Once the chosen engine which gives the

Preparing the engine for marinization. (a) The chosen engine – not a pretty sight!

(b) After a careful clean down with degreaser . . .

power required is actually at the workplace, preparations for marinizing can begin. If it is a new or reconditioned unit it will be ready for painting but if it is second-hand the first job required will be a complete clean down.

Using an old wood chisel or similar tool as a scraper, remove the excess grease and caked-on mud before washing down. One of the proprietary engine cleaners from car accessory shops will do a good job when used in conjunction with a wire brush and scraper to remove the residue of the thickest dirt and grease. Once all the surface muck is in a soluble form a spray with a hose will wash everything off.

Set up the engine for starting and if possible arrange a supply of cooling water to allow the engine to run for a slightly longer period than was possible at the

(c) . . . and a thorough hosing . . .

(d) . . . it will be ready for a test run.

breaker's yard. A gravity feed to the fuel pump will suffice for the fuel feed and a mechanical oil pressure gauge screwed directly into the sender orifice will check the oil pressure (it will usually not be possible to test this while at the breaker's yard). Run the engine and check that the oil pressure is within the limits stated in the engine manual. If everything still appears to be in good order stop the engine and allow it to cool down for a while. Unwanted items of equipment such as the exhaust manifold and engine fan (also the air compressor or exhauster on larger truck engines) can then be removed and discarded.

Unless it is quite certain that the engine is a low mileage model in excellent condition it is worth removing the sump to check the condition of the crankshaft and bearings as well as the cylinder bores. If there are no obvious signs of any damage or excess wear, a new set of big-end and main bearings can be fitted while the sump is removed. If there are signs of damage or wear it is better to discard the engine at this stage and get a replacement. Once the sump is refitted any obvious oil leaks – which should have been noted before washing down – should be dealt with using new gaskets.

The basic engine can now be painted. There are excellent anti-corrosion engine paints available from car accessory shops in a range of colours to suit individual tastes, although remember that light colours tend to show up any subsequent oil leaks. Once painted, the engine will be ready to accept the marinizing equipment.

Marinizing Equipment

The equipment required to convert a standard engine block for indirect (or fresh water) cooling will generally consist of a heat exchanger, water-cooled exhaust manifold, a raw (or sea) water pump, oil cooler, marine gearbox plus drive plate and adaptor plates, engine mounting plates and feet, and various other options such as sump pumps and power take-offs for bilge pumping and generators. Depending on the make of engine there may also be a need for other conversion items such as modified thermostat housings to allow the new pipework to connect to the existing engine system.

It is quite possible to find all this marinizing equipment second-hand through boat jumbles or in the classified pages of boat magazines, but this can lead to problems of incompatibility between parts requiring extensive pipework for connecting up. Although this will lead to an untidy looking engine it can be a big money-saver which works perfectly well. If the complete marinizing kit is bought from a company such as Lancing Marine, it can be supplied with everything required including pipework which does make for a neater job although, of course, the costs are greater.

Fitting the Parts

This is really very straightforward requiring only the most basic of engineering skills to remove the old parts and fit the new. A set of the appropriate engine gaskets for fitting the manifold and items like the thermostat housing will be needed, but if oil leaks have already been dealt with then a complete gasket set for the engine will already be available.

If a complete marinizing kit is being used then all the necessary brackets should have been provided. If the equipment has been collected second-hand then it will be necessary to make up supports for items such as oil coolers, but these are generally quite simple although it is necessary to plan the pipe runs first so that the layout of the equipment can be decided. Domestic copper pipe and solder fittings are cheap and readily available in many sizes which will make it possible to complete a very neat pipework installation without too much flexible hose trailing round the engine.

A good supply of hose clips of varying sizes to ensure that all the pipe joints are properly made will be needed. Stainless steel types are available but they cannot be tightened very far before they strip. The cheaper and stronger galvanized types which if given an occasional spray of lubricating water repellent last very well and can be tightened to a greater degree.

Of particular importance is choosing the type of hose to use; if possible always use vehicle-type hoses although these are not always easily obtainable in large sizes so reinforced clear hose works well. On the suction side of the raw water pump it is particularly important that the hose is reinforced to prevent it collapsing under suction and thereby cutting off the water flow. Some of the spiral-wound plastic hose available from chandlers actually shrinks dramatically when heated, and the temperature of the engine water is more than enough to do this. Check for this by putting a piece in a saucepan of hot water before fitting.

Heat Exchanger and Water-Cooled Exhaust Manifold

Manufacturers are turning more and more to combined heat-exchanger manifolds as the main item of marinizing equipment as these are cheaper to produce than separate units, are easier to fit and are neater.

Depending on whether the engine is a cross-flow type with the inlet manifold on the opposite side to the exhaust will decide on the amount of work required. Where the heat exchanger/manifold is opposite the inlet all that is required is to remove the old manifold from the mating face on the engine block, fit a new gasket (if a gasket is specified) and bolt on the new heat-exchanger manifold, taking care to tighten the securing nuts evenly and to the torque specified in the engine manual.

If the inlet manifold is on the same side as the exhaust it may need to be replaced with a new marine type as in many cases the old inlet manifold will not clear the new heat exchanger. On some smaller engines the inlet manifold can simply be removed, turned upside-down and after cleaning the mating faces on both the block and the old manifold, fitting a new gasket followed by both the inlet manifold and heat exchanger/manifold, again tightening the securing nuts evenly to the correct torque.

Fitting the heat exchanger and water-cooled exhaust manifold. (a) Fit the new gasket.

(b) Refit the inlet manifold (or fit a marine replacement).

(c) Fit the heat exchanger/manifold.

(d) Remove the old thermostat housing.

(e) Remove the old thermostat and replace it with a new one.

(f) Remember to use a new gasket.

(g) Fit the new thermostat housing and connect to the heat exchanger/manifold with a suitable hose.

(h) The exhaust cooling water feed pipework can be made up from copper fittings.

Oil Cooler

Oil coolers are usually mounted on brackets in convenient locations on the engine block where they can be neatly incorporated into the pipework run. At one time it was common practice to have the cooling drawn through the oil coolers before passing through the water pump, but this can dramatically cut the pump performance as the length of pipework through which the pump must draw the water becomes excessive. The coolers should therefore be installed in positions where the water is pumped through them under pressure from the pump rather than drawing the water through them.

Raw Water Pump

This is a critical item if proper cooling is to be achieved and the mounting will depend on the type of pump used. We looked in detail at the different types of pump available in Chapter 5, with each having different methods of mounting and driving. Once the pump is satisfactorily mounted the main considerations are coupling the pipework so that the inlet rather than the outlet of the pump is actually connected to the boat's sea cock (an easy mistake to make) and that the pipework runs smoothly with the minimum of sharp bends and is well supported clear of areas where physical damage can take place.

Fitting the Gearbox

There are many makes of gearbox from which to choose and all the modern types are either servo or hydraulically operated which means that lightweight single lever controls can be used. This will probably be the most expensive item on the marinizing shopping list, so if a second-hand unit can be found large savings will be made.

Different makes of gearbox require different oils and it is essential to use the correct type and grade. PRM and Twin Disc boxes use normal engine oil while Hurth and Borg Warner use automatic transmission fluid.

Mechanical gearboxes are not really worth considering as they suffer from wear, and replacement parts could end up costing the equivalent of a good hydraulic box. Adaptor plates and drive plates are available from marinizers to cover most engine and gearbox combinations – this simplifies the job as all they require is bolting on and accurate alignment.

Mounting the raw water pump will depend on the type of pump used. This high-speed type fits to the engine water pump pulley.

Fitting the gearbox. (a) Some engines require a weight on the flywheel for smooth running when used in marine form . . .

(b) . . . but they all require a drive plate.

(c) The flywheel housing is fitted next . . .

(d) . . . followed by the gearbox itself, which needs careful alignment in the drive plate.

(e) The complete gearbox assembly.

Outdrives

These can give a saving on stern gear and gearbox as they perform both functions. There are fewer adaptor parts required and they are fairly easy to fit (after ensuring that the transom is strong enough to take the weight and thrust).

Engine Feet and Mounts

Any engine installation on a pleasure boat will need to be on flexible mounts otherwise vibrations will cause great discomfort. The only type of boat which can use a solid installation is the very heavy steel or wooden working boat where the construction of the boat is solid enough to absorb vibrations. A modern and fairly lightweight craft will vibrate throughout if the engine is installed without flexible mounts.

When buying a complete marinizing kit it will often be possible to use the standard engine feet for mounting the engine as the marinizer will have designed the package to suit these. When building a DIY one-off it may be necessary to design feet for the engine, but with simple welding skills (or knowing a friendly welder) fabrication is fairly easy. The flexible mounts chosen for mounting the engine will decide how successful the job of preventing vibration will be. It is best to consult an expert in this field (such as R and D Marine) for advice on the correct mountings to use for the size and type of engine.

Remove the old vehicle mounts if new marine mounts are to be fitted.

The last job on the marinizing list is to fill the engine with fresh oil.

Shaft Couplings

To allow a certain amount of flexibility between shaft and gearbox flange a flexible coupling will be needed. These vary greatly in price and type – probably the cheapest are the R and D Marine units which are excellent and work very well, while the most expensive will be the 'Aquadrive' from Halyard Marine. These are the 'Rolls Royce' of the coupling world and not only stop vibration being transmitted down the shaft but also allow a large degree of misalignment between engine and shaft which can make installation much simpler. They also incorporate a thrust bearing to take the thrust from the propeller via a heavy flange bolted to the engine beds rather than through the gearbox. However, they are expensive and excellent results can still be obtained by careful installation of R and D units.

SUMMARY

- All so-called marine engines on sale today are derived from vehicle or industrial units.

- Spares are always cheaper from the local vehicle dealer than the marine engineers.

- Breaker's yards are a good source of cheap power plants for boats.

- Marinizing is well within the scope of the average DIY mechanic.

9
ON-BOARD TOOLS
AND SPARES

As stated right at the start of this book, self-sufficiency afloat is a part of good seamanship, and this means being able to cope with any minor breakdowns which occur while under way. To be able to do this not only requires the right tools for the job, it is also essential to carry a spares kit covering the items most likely to fail in service.

The Toolkit

If a motor boat should break down at sea it is the skipper who must try to rectify the problem and get the boat under way again so that it can return to safety under its own power.

Any craft which puts to sea, however small, should always have some means of auxiliary propulsion as a back-up against the unexpected breakdown. This is true whether it be a simple pair of oars for the smallest of dinghies, a small outboard motor on a swing-down bracket on medium-sized cruisers, an inboard wing engine on larger models or twin engines on any size of craft. This ensures that when the worst happens the vessel can continue under power without resorting to calls for help from outside sources. It is extremely selfish as well as very poor

seamanship to go to sea relying on others to come to the rescue and who may possibly have to risk their lives just because the vessel is not properly equipped.

Even the best equipped and maintained craft can suffer from breakdowns at sea due to any number of unexpected causes, and although the back-up motor will keep the boat going (assuming it has not also failed due perhaps to a common fuel fault) it will be at greatly reduced speed. There are few twin-engined craft which can maintain planing speed when one engine has stopped, so at best the trip will be slowed down very considerably.

Often the fault is quite minor and can be repaired in a few minutes if the correct tools are available, but if these have been left in the boot of the car or are not comprehensive enough to cover all the various bolt-head sizes in common use, it is not only inconvenient but also extremely frustrating, especially if both engines are out of action and an RT call for help must be made.

The problem with boat engines and equipment today is the differing nut and bolt types used. Whitworth sizes are still very common especially on older engines, stern gear and American equipment. AF sizes were standard on most British engines until a few years ago with many thousands still in service. However, metric sizes are now commonly used on all modern equipment as companies fall into line with European practice. This means that three sets of tools are necessary to cover all the bolt sizes likely to be encountered on an average boat. Good-quality socket sets usually have a selection of each type but spanner sets need to be bought separately.

In recent years Richmond tools have overcome this problem to a large extent by introducing the Metrinch 6WD system of sockets and spanners which are fairly revolutionary in their way as they fit all types of nut or bolt head. For instance the 13mm socket or spanner will also fit the ½in AF and ¼in Whitworth bolt meaning that the set of tools can consist of only 30 per cent of the standard type while still covering the full range of sizes. They work on the flat of the bolt head rather than the corners as is the case with the standard socket or spanner and so avoid the problem of rounded off corners on the bolt head which often occurs with worn and ill-fitting spanners. The design allows the tools to be a looser fit on the bolt heads than is normal with standard tools, and for experienced mechanics this takes some getting used to. Other than this these sets are ideal as a basis for the on-board toolkit as they reduce the overall number of tools required.

In any boat there is the odd nut or bolt which is outside the range of the standard toolkit and this is where a good-quality adjustable spanner will often prove useful. In fact, it is worth having a set of adjustables to cover all sizes as they can be very useful when an additional spanner of a particular size is needed.

Small-sized spanners are also useful especially when bleeding a fuel system, and a cheap socket set with very small sizes is also very handy for getting into awkward spots where the standard set cannot reach.

A large Stilson pipe-wrench is yet another excellent multi-function tool which will adjust to very large sizes to unscrew items such as stern glands or propeller nuts, while the trusty 'Mole' vice-grip wrench, pliers, side-cutters and long-nose pliers will all come in handy at some stage.

A selection of hammers are worth investing in, from a 1kg (2·5lb) 'club' hammer to a light ball peen. A selection of screwdrivers including slot, Phillips, and Posidrive in a variety of sizes will be almost essential.

Hexagon-head Allen keys are usually required at some stage and sets can now be bought which fit into socket-set drives making them very much more versatile.

A hacksaw and junior hacksaw have many uses and should be considered essential,

An example of a Metrinch open-ended spanner.

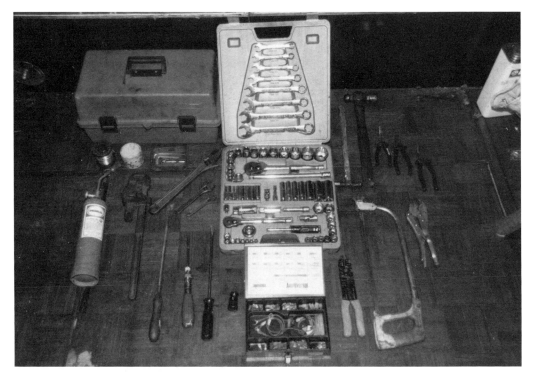

A good, basic, on-board toolkit.

while a 12-volt electrical soldering iron will make light electrical repairs a possibility. A blow lamp, solder and flux will also increase the scope for plumbing and heavy electrical repairs.

Buying tools is still very much a case of 'getting what you pay for' and it is worth investing in the best possible set available although it must be said that moderately priced socket sets will usually offer good service as will spanners. However, with screwdrivers it is worth paying a little extra for good-quality types which will last without the points breaking or bending.

The ideal practice is to have a separate set of tools permanently on the boat, but as this can prove expensive when another set is required in the car and a further set at home, it is feasible to have one set but to always ensure that it is on board before beginning any trip.

Once the tools have been purchased it is pointless to throw them into the bilges to rust away. They should be stored in a proper tool-box ready for immediate use. There are many good-quality plastic boxes on the market at reasonable prices which are ideal for boat use, and if the tools are given an occasional spray with lubricating water repellent they will remain in good condition ready for immediate use when problems arise.

On-board Toolkit

Socket set – AF, metric and
　　　　　Whitworth sizes
Spanners, open-ended and ring – AF,
　　　　metric and Whitworth sizes
(Or all above combined in Metrinch set.)
'Stilson' pipe-wrench – large
Adjustable spanners – small, medium
　　　　　　　　　and large
Vice-grip wrench
Pliers – standard and long nose
Side-cutters
Allen keys – imperial and metric
Screwdrivers – slot, Phillips and
　　　　　　　Posidrive
Hammers – 1kg (2·5lb), club and light
　　　　　ball peen
Hacksaws – standard and junior
Blow lamp – preferably gas
12V Electrical soldering iron
Heavy-duty plastic tool-box

The On-board Spares Kit

When compiling a list of spares for the boat, the first thing to decide is how comprehensive the kit will be – this will be decided by the length of cruises and the ultimate destinations. For instance, a boat venturing far abroad will require a more comprehensive kit than one which stays on the inland waterways or coast of Britain.

The obvious place to start compiling the kit is with the engine. Assuming the boat is remaining within the UK or the near Continent it will not be necessary to carry such spares as pistons and valves as a major breakdown involving such items as these will usually curtail the cruise and involve professional assistance. However,

items which suffer from fatigue and eventual failure such as raw water pump impellers, and hoses and drive belts, should be carried and stored ready for use. Self-amalgamating tape is ideal for making running repairs on split hoses on engine cooling pipes and other areas of the boat, so a large roll (which is available from chandlers) is worth carrying. Some marine engines require the water pump pipework to be removed before a belt drive can be replaced which makes an otherwise simple job rather more time consuming. It is often possible to tape a spare belt into place behind the pipework and out of the way of the running belt so that it can quickly be fitted in an emergency without removing the pipework.

A tube of instant gasket sealant will always come in handy to cure oil leaks when the correct gasket is not on board, and added to this should be a roll of gasket paper so that gaskets can be fabricated on the spot.

Fuel filters should be included as a blocked fuel line caused by stirred up sediment in the tank in rough weather will quickly stop a diesel engine. Some spare fuel delivery tubing for replacing fractured pipework, and compression joints to cover every area of the fuel system are useful and make a reliable and permanent repair. A fuel-lift pump overhaul kit including a replacement diaphragm is a good addition, although a complete spare pump is better as it can be changed in a matter of minutes in the event of failure.

A spare injector is a worthwhile item as although a single faulty injector will not usually stop an engine it will cause a loss of power and a smoky exhaust, and may lead to mechanical damage if allowed to drip fuel into the bore. Another essential is a set of spare injector pipes in case one should fracture. It may be possible to carry one long pipe and bend it into shape to suit the faulty pipe, but great care must be taken to ensure that the pipe is not weakened during bending and for the price of a full set it is hardly worth taking the risk.

Naturally a plentiful supply of lubricating oils of the correct grade for engine and gearbox will also be needed as well as more than sufficient fuel for the trip with a good margin for safety. Running out of fuel at sea indicates a total lack of forethought and planning and is the height of bad seamanship!

The electrical system will need spare fuses of all sizes plus a supply of wire of different gauges for emergency repairs in the case of damage or burning. As we have seen, proper crimp terminals make totally reliable joints, and these are available in complete kits with a selection of terminals and a crimping tool. Some insulating tape and electrician's flux-cored solder will often come in handy as well.

Every owner will have their own additions to the list and the items mentioned are by no means comprehensive, but they should form the basis of the spares kit which can be extended to cover the needs of the individual boat depending on where it is cruising, how far and for how long.

On-board Spares Kit

Engine spares

Drive belts for pumps and alternators
Water cooling hoses and self-amalgamating tape
Raw water pump impellers
Fuel filters
Instant gasket sealant plus a roll of gasket paper
Lubricating oil for the engine and gearbox
Fuel delivery piping
Fuel-lift pump kit or spare pump
Copper tube and solder fittings
At least one spare injector
Set of injector pipes or one long enough to reach any injector

Electrical spares

Fuses in all sizes
Wire of different gauges
Insulating tape
Flux-cored solder

SUMMARY

- A comprehensive toolkit is an essential part of the equipment of every boat fitted with an engine.

- The kit must cover every size of nut, bolt and screw on the vessel.

- The spares kit must be comprehensive enough to cover the needs of the boat and its expected cruising range.

- The spares kit should include a full range of lubricating oils and greases.

- Sufficient fuel for the trip with a good margin for safety should be considered an essential part of the on-board spares kit!

SOME USEFUL FUEL CONSUMPTION COMPARISONS

- 2-stroke petrol ....10hp per gallon per hour
- 4-stroke petrol ....15hp per gallon per hour
- naturally aspirated diesel ....20hp per gallon per hour
- turbo-charged diesel ....23hp per gallon per hour

Although only a rough guide, the figures make estimating maximum fuel consumption easy. Divide the rated maximum horse-power of the engine by the figure appropriate to the type of engine as listed.
ie 100hp diesel will achieve approximately 5 gallons per hour at maximum power. (100 ÷ 20 = 5).

GLOSSARY

After-cooler Similar in design to a heat exchanger, the after- (or inter-) cooler, cools and condenses the compressed intake air provided by a turbo-charger by further boosting power output.

Agglomerator A fine fuel filter which collects tiny drops of water and combines them until they are large enough to sink to the bottom of the filter body for draining.

Arc Welding A process involving flux-coated metal rods which melt and fuse with other metals when brought into close proximity, so that an electric arc is formed due to the current supplied by the transformer. The flux coating forms a gas as the rod melts and excludes oxygen from the welded joint to prevent the metals becoming brittle.

Calorifier A domestic water-storage tank with a heating coil within which is fed with hot water from the fresh cooling system of the engine, providing free hot water from waste heat produced by the engine.

Camshaft Running at half engine speed the camshaft operates the opening and closing of the inlet and exhaust valves.

Compression Joint A mechanical joint used in pipe-work to provide a perfect seal which can be opened and resealed many times without losing the effectiveness of the seal.

Core Plug A plug fitted into the outer water jacket of an engine block. Its purpose is to prevent the engine block from cracking by pushing out under the pressure of ice when the engine has frozen through lack of antifreeze.

Crankshaft The component which converts the up/down movement of the pistons into the rotary motion of the output shaft.

Crimp Terminal A cable end-fitting which provides the means of making a professional quality joint. It is available in a variety of sizes and styles to suit different applications. Low-cost kits complete with crimping tool are available from car accessory shops.

Direct Injection A term used to describe engines where the fuel is sprayed directly on top of the piston.

Direct Cooling A method of water cooling where the water from the river or sea is pumped directly around the engine block before being expelled, usually via the exhaust.

External Combustion The process of producing heat energy from an external source away from the cylinder of an engine, resulting in massive heat loss and minimal efficiency. Used in steam engines.

Four-stroke Cycle A series of four strokes of a piston, two up and two down which form the complete combustion cycle of a

GLOSSARY

four-stroke engine, requiring two revolutions of the crankshaft.

Fuel-lift Pump A mechanically operated pump driven from the camshaft which lifts fuel from the tank and passes it into the fuel system via the filters.

Gas Oil The standard fuel for diesel engines, with a higher flash point than petrol, which almost eradicates the risk of explosion, making it highly suitable for marine use.

Heater Plugs Cold start devices incorporating a heating coil. They are screwed into every combustion chamber of the engine to warm the air within and assist with cold starting.

Hot-bulb Engine A design of internal combustion engine developed and commercially produced by Herbert Akroyd Stuart, which many people consider to be the first real diesel engine and often referred to as a 'semi-diesel'.

Impeller The moving part of a rotary pump which moves the liquid. It may be made of metal or a flexible material such as the rubber or nitrile used in Jabsco raw water pumps.

Indirect Cooling A method of water cooling where the water from the river or sea passes through tubes in a heat exchanger which transfers the heat from the fresh water circulating through the block.

Indirect Injection A term used to describe engines with pre-combustion chambers.

Injection Pump This meters the amount of fuel to be sprayed into the cylinder at any given throttle setting, and the time of injection on the combustion cycle.

Injector Also referred to as an atomizer. They are a self-sealing valve which

atomizes a precise metered amount of fuel and sprays it into the combustion chamber under pressure from the injection pump.

Internal Combustion The process of producing heat energy from fuel within the cylinder of an engine, which reduces heat loss and provides maximum efficiency from the burned fuel. Used in diesel and petrol engines.

Master Spline The large spline on an injection-pump drive spindle which ensures that the spindle can only be inserted into the drive in the correct alignment.

Mig Welding This works on the same electrical principle as the arc welder but uses continuous flexible wire fed from a motor-driven drum in place of rods, and a canister of inert gas to exclude oxygen from the joint in place of flux.

Olive A metal ring, usually of brass or copper, used to seal a compression pipe joint.

Piston Ring A split ring which fits in a groove in the wall of a piston and forms a seal against the cylinder wall.

Power-to-weight Ratio The output power of an engine compared to its weight. A heavy engine with a low power output would have a lower power-to-weight ratio than a lightweight unit with a high power output.

Pre-combustion Chamber A small chamber off the main cylinder where fuel is sprayed in at the ignition point and which offers smoother running at the cost of slightly reduced fuel economy.

Raw water Pump This is used to draw water from the river or sea for engine cooling, and may be used in both direct- and indirect-cooled systems.

Sedimenter A coarse filter used to remove large quantities of water and dirt from fuel before the fuel enters the fine filter.

Spark Plug An electrical igniter used to assist the combustion process within petrol engines.

Sump The oil reservoir at the bottom of the engine, usually a pressed-steel fabrication.

Thermostart A cold-start device mounted in the inlet manifold, utilizing a heating coil which opens a fuel valve to allow fuel onto the coil. The fuel is ignited and the flames are drawn into the cylinders to assist with cold starting.

Turbo-charger A turbine-powered air pump driven by exhaust gases, which raises the intake pressure to provide greater power output.

Two-stroke Cycle A series of two strokes of a piston, one up and one down which form the complete combustion cycle of a two-stroke engine, requiring one revolution of the crankshaft.

Voltage Drop The difference between voltage measured at a battery and at the end of a long section of cable.

INDEX